TINFOIL HAT NOT INCLUDED

conspiracy theories in art and practice

JOSEPH
E. GREEN

Tinfoil Hat Not Included:
Conspiracy Theories in Art and Practice

JOSEPH E. GREEN

Cover image by Barbara Zandoval courtesy of Unsplash

DEDICATION

For
John and Mae

CONTENTS

Introduction

INTRODUCTION

What is all the fuss with conspiracy theories these days? After the QAnon rebellion at the capitol, encouraged by the former President Donald Trump, and in the midst of the Pandemic, or the *Plandemic* as some chose to call it, the world seems steeped in conspiracy in thought and action. Major news organizations seem to agree: *Conspiracy theorists are on the loose! Fueled by the Internet and ready for violence, both left-wing and right-wing extremist science deniers lie in wait to dismantle society and poison the youth.*

But while there are, as always, dangerous folks out there, it is the incoherent messaging in the media that should give one pause about accepting everything at face value. Just one example: Everyone is expected to agree that ordinary people should listen to scientists and not do their own research, but also simultaneously listen to Bill Gates, who is not a scientist but does his own research. The difference seems to be that Gates is very rich and you are not.

It has been strange to be in this field (as it were) of conspiracy research for some twenty years and then watch it go mainstream. I have sometimes jokingly referred to it as "Our Thing," the way Tony Soprano referred to the business of mobsterdom. It got *really* strange when certain people who were only or mostly known to those in Our Thing suddenly went viral - Alex Jones, Roger Stone, and the like - generally the worst people you would ever want to have representing anything.

What happened, as far as I can see it, is that a formerly specialized field got turned into amateur hour. You might think that's an odd observation, but the fact of the matter is that many people who have been tagged with the "conspiracy theorist" label are highly respected professional people. For example, when ordinary folks think of JFK conspiracy researchers, they probably picture that famous *It's Always Sunny in Philadelphia* meme of a guy standing in front of a board with all sorts of crazy arrows pointing in all directions, insisting that Pepe Silvia is the key to everything. There's some of that, I suppose. But there's also Dr. Cyril Wecht, who is more or less the most famous pathologist in the world (and who has his JD in addition to his medical degree). There's Dr. Gary Aguilar, a world-class surgical ophthalmologist. There's Dr. Peter Dale Scott, who taught at Berkeley and also served as a Canadian diplomat for many years.

This is not to say one has to have a university imprimatur to be taken seriously, or that they can't be wrong, but the point is that these folks aren't basement dwellers watching YouTube videos. These are serious professional people who saw something awry, did some investigation on their own, and found big problems with the official story. And the people who started looking into these things did so because they felt that they needed to do the work that their government was refusing to do. I was fortunate to be in correspondence with Vince Salandria for the last several years of his life, and he was the sanest man I ever knew. He continually referred to himself as a "simple Philadelphia lawyer," but he also figured out something was wrong the weekend of the Kennedy assassination – instantly. He started working to find the truth the day after Lee Harvey Oswald's public murder.

You have to be built a certain way to pursue this line of inquiry now, and you can imagine what it was like in 1963. There is a detailed illustration about this process – and what it can cost, professionally and personally – in

Joseph McBride's wonderful book *Into the Nightmare: My Search for the Killers of President John F. Kennedy and Officer J.D. Tippit.*

The fact remains: If you are motivated to find the truth, then you have to go where the evidence takes you. I didn't want to know that Oswald didn't shoot Kennedy, and I certainly didn't want to find out that the RFK assassination was a conspiracy, and that the MLK assassination was a conspiracy, and that the Malcolm X assassination was a conspiracy, and that the Jonestown story as people know it is completely wrong, and that Ted Kennedy survived multiple assassination attempts, and so on. It's not my fault that the government keeps murdering its own citizens. And there's no reason why people should find it all that irrational. We know for a fact that the U.S. government was involved in the overthrow of Salvador Allende, the murder of Patrice Lumumba, the support and then later removal of Rafael Trujillo, and there are documents galore indicting COINTELPRO for their work killing black and native leaders and destroying the Black Panthers from within. We know the government set up Leonard Peltier and murdered Fred Hampton. Our tax dollars pay for enormous operations dedicated to subverting and killing leaders in other countries. Is it that much of a stretch to think it might be used domestically?

This is especially true when considering the mental state of the men who have made up the intelligence services in this country. For example, you may not be aware of a certain Major Carleton Stevens Coon, but in 1943 he provided a report to the head of the Office of Strategic Services (OSS), "Wild Bill" Donovan which advocated for maintaining America's dominance essentially by any means necessary. The OSS was the forerunner of the CIA, instituted in 1947. Major Coon's report told the story:

> We cannot be sure that the clear and objective scholars who study the existing social systems, and draw blueprints for a society to suit our technology, will always be heard, or that their plans will be put into operations. We can almost be sure this will not be the case. Therefore, some other power, some third class of individuals aside from the leaders and scholars, must exist, and this third class must have the task of thwarting mistakes, diagnosing areas of political world disequilibrium, and nipping causes of potential disturbances in the bud...it must either be a power unto itself or given the broadest discretionary powers by the highest human authorities.

What does that sound like to you? And this is **1943**.

As is perhaps evident from the quoted passage, Major Coon ironically had some retrograde ideas about racial purity, which he put into his books *The Races of Europe* and *The Origins of Races*, the latter of which appeared in 1962. A Harvard PhD in anthropology, he was friends with Ashley Montague for years although they eventually broke over his lunatic racial theories. And yet his way of thinking is evident in precisely the colonial practices that link the early conquistadors to American incursions into Vietnam, Korea, Latin America, and Africa, and of course in the territory once called Turtle Island – by its indigenous inhabitants – and now referred to as the United States of America.

***

You will notice that when a typical journalist working for a big news organization starts to discuss ideologically "dangerous" issues, they will spend much energy raising psychological explanations without ever attempting to deal with the facts. That's because if they raise factual issues, two things happen: (1) the journalist has to acquire some familiarity with those facts, and (2) the process lends credence to those who question them. It is far easier to libel investigators as psychologically damaged and then cite authorities who pooh-pooh all such notions.

One recent example is the journalist Mike Rothschild, who has made a career out of debunking conspiracies in his books *The Storm is Upon Us* and *The World's Worst Conspiracies*. In an article about QAnon followers and the efforts to ban them from participating in public dialogues, he writes about the key role played by QAnon in the belief of many that there are high-level pedophilia rings in modern society. : "And since child trafficking and pedophilia, mostly connected to Jeffrey Epstein and Hollywood, have been a part of QAnon lore since the beginning, QAnon helped drive that as well."[i] Note that Rothschild makes no attempt to verify whether those beliefs are credible; they are taken to be absurd at face value, because they are associated with QAnon believers. While this might seem like a safe bet – believing that Trump is going to retake office with the help of a resurrected John F. Kennedy Jr. is an unlikely prospect – it isn't *definitive*. After all, Jeffrey Epstein was a sexual predator, and one would have to be very incurious indeed to think that (1) Epstein did nothing illegal, and (2) had no help in procuring girls for the powerful people he was associated with. England recently had a scandal of its own with Sir Jimmy Saville, whose own contacts reached into the Royal family.

The basic problem is this: truth cannot be resolved relative to the sanity of the speaker. Highly sane and intelligent people make mistakes, and occasionally madmen reveal insights. The tools of demarcation have to finer than simply labeling people we dislike.

Just for purposes of demonstration, here is one example of why journalists cannot get into what happened in these cases. Let's take one detail from the Martin Luther King assassination.

James Earl Ray was the guy who allegedly killed Martin Luther King. He didn't, but that's the guy the government said did the shooting. There are hundreds of crazy things about this case, but as promised I am going to pick just one.

When MLK was shot to death, an enormous manhunt began for the assassin. Before this event, James Earl Ray had been a petty criminal. His father had been one as well. (I interviewed one of Ray's brothers, who had no trouble talking about the "family business.")

According to the government, after shooting King, Ray ran outside the building he was in, threw the rifle and a whole bunch of incriminating material – including his prison radio and his underwear – right on the sidewalk before fleeing. (A key witness stated that the pile was placed there a few minutes *before* the shooting, but never mind that.)

Ray escaped. He then proceeded to elude law enforcement's manhunt for months. Please note that Ray was not a master of disguise, nor was he a genius. According to the FBI, Ray was also a methamphetamine addict, so he also presumably had to score at various times while on the run. Despite this, Ray managed to leave the country numerous times. In fact, when he was arrested, it was in London's Heathrow Airport by *Scotland Yard.*

Think about that for a minute.

But the real kicker in all of this was that in the months after the assassination, Ray at one point went to Montreal, where he managed to obtain four different identification cards. All four of the identities were stolen from real people who existed and lived in the Montreal area, and they all looked like him.

Reminder: this is 1968. And James Earl Ray was not James Bond.

So how did Ray, between shots of meth, raise the cash necessary to obtain these identities, and who did he get them from? There wasn't an internet to look up people who looked like him and print out identity cards.

Who had the capability in 1968 to (1) do a search for people in the same city who resembled each other enough for Ray to pass as them, and then (2) obtain identification for those different people that Ray could use?

This is one tiny detail. When you start looking at these cases, stuff like this pops out everywhere.

***

When a police detective is investigating a typical murder, associations between people are considered a significant clue. This is because most murders are not worthy of being solved by Sherlock Holmes. They are mostly crimes of passion between people who used to love one another or crimes of necessity between people who are involved in drugs or other crime together. If the wife gets shot, the husband probably did it. If a guy gets shot in a drug deal gone wrong, it was probably someone who wanted the money or drugs more than he did. Associations are important.

But this reasoning gets thrown away whenever someone important gets murdered. If you applied standard cop logic to the crime of (say) the President getting killed, then you would look at associations - the Vice President, the Joint Chiefs – and then means, motive, and opportunity.

Nope. Not when it comes to presidents. It is wrong and stupid to even ask the question. It is totally impertinent.

Why?

There is no logical reason.

What follows are a few essays that I've written that go into the topic of conspiracy as a concept, rather than the specific details of particular conspiracies. Some have appeared previously in other outlets, such as Jim DiEugenio's *Kennedys and King* website, as well as the print publications *Deep Truth Journal* and *Garrison Magazine*. The last couple of essays explore some of the ways conspiracy wanders into the history of Hollywood films and my own experiences in that arena.

I hope they add to the conversation that should be had in the mainstream, without the standard shouting matches that occur between people convinced that the other side are either "sheeple" or lunatics. There's no reason to ever accept hard binaries in this conversation, particularly during a time in which we're all learning that even biological systems don't necessarily use hard binaries.

Thanks for reading.

-Joe G., 6/9/2021

"A few months ago I told the American people I did not trade arms for hostages. My heart and my best intentions still tell me that's true, but the facts and the evidence tell me that it is not."

-Ronald Reagan

"People like to say, I don't want to believe in conspiracies. Look - I've got the minutes of their meetings. What else do you want?"

-BBC reporter Greg Palast

WHAT GENTLEMEN DON'T ASK OTHER GENTLEMEN

Now I would not normally be in the business of quoting the National Review, but these are far from normal times. Entitled "The Breaking of Stephen Colbert," and written by Peter Spiliakos, the piece discusses an incident in which the comedian Jon Stewart visited the Stephen Colbert television program and endorse the Wuhan lab-leak theory. This is remarkable in media terms because the lab-leak theory was endorsed by Donald Trump, and is therefore opposed by all good liberals on doctrinaire grounds.

I have no particular opinion about the lab-leak theory, and think it is relatively unimportant compared with the state overreach involved in the reaction to the pandemic. What is important, in my view, is to continue viewing all topics in view of whatever evidence can be obtained — not which political party espouses it. Although most of my political opinions can be nominally aligned with liberalism, in truth I am vastly further to the left than anyone allowed airtime in these United States.

For his part, in this article Peter Spiliakos observes: "In the wider America, the vast majority either believe in the lab-leak theory or are agnostic on the subject. But for the Very Online Left, the lab-leak theory isn't about true or false. It's about in-group vs. out-group, and anyone who volunteers that the lab-leak theory might be true is part of the out-group."[ii]

As you will see from what follows, this language mirrors my own in its analysis of how conspiracy thinking is treated in the mainstream. And while I would never have imagined quoting something from the National Review with approval, I have to give credit where it's due. OK, now the piece starts for real.

You may know the name Scott Simon. Mr. Simon has been the host of the program *Weekend Edition* on National Public Radio since 1985, and thus his voice is very familiar to millions of people. His job title, if you look it up, is investigative journalist.

A few years before Simon began hosting that program, on March 30, 1981, President Ronald Reagan was shot just outside the Washington Hilton Hotel after speaking to a labor organization. The accused assassin John Hinckley, Jr., (referred to as a "deranged drifter" by the History Channel) was tackled by police at the scene. Hinckley, it is alleged, also shot three other people: then-Press Secretary James Brady, D.C. cop Thomas

Delahanty, and Secret Service agent Tim McCarthy. Oddly, Hinckley is said to have used a .22-caliber pistol in the assassination attempt, a seemingly peculiar choice for someone with deadly intent. However, he used "Devastator" bullets, so named because they were said to "explode" upon impact beyond the ordinary expansion of such projectiles. For what it's worth, only the shot that hit Brady exploded in the advertised manner, according to the surgeons who saved his life.

I do not wish, however, to get into whether or not Hinckley actually fired the shots that hit these men. The full video of the attack is available online to be seen by anyone and there are several anomalies in it. Let's assume that he was, as is recorded in the history books, the actual shooter, on a provisional basis, because I have other fish to fry at the moment.

John Hinckley, Jr. is the son of Jack Hinckley, now deceased, but a former oil executive. The Hinckley family, it turns out, had been longtime friends of the Bush family. In fact, the Hinckleys had contributed money to Bush's very first Senate campaign, in March of 1970. It also turned out that Neil Bush, one of the sons of Vice-President Bush, had dinner plans with John Hinckley's brother which was to happen the day after the shooting. (These plans were canceled.)

So this is a bit strange, no?

25

Let's be clear. **I am not saying that VP George Bush ordered a hit on President Ronald Reagan so he could then vault into the top job.** I am saying, however, that the question *needs* to be asked. In any standard attempted homicide investigation, this question *would* be asked. If the CEO of a chocolate factory were shot at, and it turned out the shooter was a close relative of the person next in line for CEO, I *guarantee* the question would be asked.

Scott Simon – erstwhile investigative reporter for National Public Radio – had the chance to ask the question when he did a long piece on Bush shortly after the attempted assassination. During this time, mainstream news stories mentioned the Hinckley-Bush connection – when they did so at all – in passing, as a coincidence not worthy of notice. When Simon was asked why no reporters did their due diligence on this question, he replied: "That may be something that gentlemen just don't ask gentlemen."

So here's the thing. I don't like that. I don't like that there are certain questions one is not supposed to ask because of some sort of courtly brotherhood. Where the government and a free press is concerned, I don't believe in *not asking the question*. Especially for someone whose alleged profession is investigative journalism. The question isn't out of bounds – quite the contrary. It leaps out to anyone with an ounce of sense.

Now let's leap forward in history a little bit. All the way to September 11, 2001. George Bush's son George ("Dubya") The Attack on America, as CNN called it. On October 11, 2001, Scott Simon wrote an editorial for the Wall Street Journal entitled " Even Pacifists Must Support This War." In this essay, Simon encouraged war protesters to stand down as America prepared for righteous vengeance upon Osama bin Laden and his evil minions. Simon closed his piece by saying: "Only American (and British) power can stop more killing in the world's skyscrapers, pizza parlors, embassies, bus stations, ships, and airplanes...It is better to sacrifice our ideals rather than ask others to die for them."

It's presumably easier for those who lack ideals. Needless to say, the absurd war that commenced (with help from Judith Miller of the New York Times and various other cheerleaders) resulted in untold deaths and injuries, the eventual capture of Saddam Hussein, and the restoration of the world's opium market via Afghanistan, which the Taliban had successfully suppressed.

The point is not to bury Scott Simon. The point is to see just how embedded the position of kowtowing to leadership is in this country. Simon works for NPR, which is typically identified with liberal Democratic thinking in America, although this is a bit of a joke in leftist circles, as it is sometimes referred to as National Petroleum Radio. Be that as it may, Simon is not a lunatic or an ideologue; instead, he appears to be someone one could have a conversation with productively. And yet, in two crucial instances, he failed his duties as a journalist in colossal, spectacular fashion.

I am quite sure that many millions of people have enjoyed his weekend program and derived pleasure from the stories he has reported on. Unfortunately, a reporter who cannot ask the difficult questions when called upon to do so, or ask why war is necessary following a highly dubious terrorist attack with a highly dubious administration in power, isn't an investigative journalist.

It used to be said sometimes that the John F. Kennedy assassination was the "third rail" of American politics. That is, investigating that murder was untouchable, and anyone who did quickly found themselves in trouble – mostly social shunning, but also occasionally legal or worse. However, since 1963, the third rail has become so expansive – as the government continues to commit crimes against its citizens – that any news program of today begins from such absurd premises that often it plays out as a grim comedy. No wonder people reject the news they're given and reach out for other sources. They can sense that a major media which cannot tell them truth on so many issues obviously cannot be trusted about life or death decisions. Which also means some of those people grab on to nonsensical ideas put out by conscienceless hucksters who – in 2016 – arrived in politics like a rotten carcass. For many people, Trump is a "straight shooter" which makes them feel heard, after so many journalists and politicians wrapped up in the immense corruption that has been at play since November 22, 1963. Of course, Trump brings a different corruption, with different players, and brought no solutions to bear. Unfortunately, unless the establishment authorities are willing to do a deep dive into their history – a highly unpleasant prospect for them – nothing will change for the better in America.

It's called thieves get rich
And saints get shot
It's called God don't answer prayers a lot

Stephen Sondheim "Now You Know"

Some of those who work forces
Are the same that burn crosses

Rage Against the Machine, "Killing in the Name of"

IS THE STATE NEUTRAL?

The June 2021 issue of the magazine Popular Mechanics contained a cover story by Joshua Pease entitled "You've Been Conditioned to Believe Conspiracy Theories. Or Have You?!" This is hardly the only such article by the mainstream press to tackle the "problem" of conspiracy theories, but it provides a handy template for analysis.

First: it never defines what a conspiracy theory is supposed to be. The concept has always been spongy. The article proposes the dictionary definition of "conspiracy" - two or more people conspiring together - but never attempts to find out what the two words together mean with any precision. (My old friend and mentor John Judge used to point out that conspiracy means "to breathe together" in Latin – and that some people have better breath than others.) The article does, however, trot out the same person who always gets quoted in these articles - Michael Shermer of Skeptic Magazine. More on him later.

Here are a few issues brought up in the article to explain why people go awry thinking about conspiracy theories:

1. **Proportionality bias**: the idea that a catastrophic event must be a result of an equally important or powerful cause. So it's too simple to believe that 9/11 was simply the result of organized hijackers led by a man in a cave, but must involve George Bush because he is "important." To bolster this analysis, the author tells the story of the Great Chicago Fire, in which a community's xenophobic response became centered on one Irish immigrant.

2. **One conspiracy theory leads to another**: the aforementioned Shermer helpfully points out that if someone believes in one conspiracy theory, they become more likely to believe another. He is quoted in the article as saying, "People who believe Princess Diana was assassinated by a secret cabal are also more likely to believe she faked her own death. Those can't both be true." He is apparently asserting that there are people who believe both of those statements, although he presents no evidence for this.

3. **Negative evidence**: Shermer says that there would be a paper trail for all government malfeasance - just as there is for Guantanamo Bay, there should be papers available for other conspiracies such as Area 51 or 9/11.

Ok, let's take a look at these.

Proportionality Bias

The author of the article engages here in what I like to call the Malcolm Gladwell/Thomas Friedman school of **reasoning by anecdote**. Friedman usually makes large pronouncements about human nature based on a story his chauffeur tells him on the way to the bank, while Gladwell will tell a story about how there was once a dog stuck in a tree, which has mind-blowing evolutionary implications, and therefore human nature proves whatever inane thesis he's been paid to defend. The very simple response to this is that one does not generally derive general conclusions from single events. The fact that there was some xenophobia in the Great Chicago Fire does not translate to a general rule that xenophobia plays a role in conspiracy theories. Xenophobia as an aspect to human nature plays a role in all sorts of ways - it often shows up in public schools, for example. Are public schools therefore connected to conspiracy theories?

One Conspiracy Leads to Another

This is true, actually, and the FBI explained why. An FBI Memo released on May 30, 2019 stated that one reason people believe in conspiracy theories is because of "the illegal, antidemocratic, or harmful activities by high level government officials and political elites." **In other words, sometimes people believe in conspiracy theories because there are in fact conspiracies!** With regard to Shermer's specific example, I do not believe that there are people who believe that Diana is both murdered and faked her death and Shermer provides no evidence of anyone who does. If you walk into any university department in any subject and pick a topic, you will find differences of opinion about that topic within the department. Some of those differences will get nasty. So what?

To be fair to Shermer, let's say that what he really means is that people believe "weird things," in his parlance, on the basis of flimsy or contradictory or just plain zero evidence. That is true. But it is also true in every single human endeavor, *including science*. Lots of scientific theories survived for decades on the basis of little to no evidence whatsoever. In addition, almost every scientist who ever changed history was thought of as a crank or an idiot before being proven correct. There are also a great many more scientists who turned out to actually be cranks or idiots. **Many are called, few are chosen.** The fact that some person might have strange ideas about number theory doesn't mean that numbers don't exist.

Shermer-style logic means that you can tar everyone with a single brush, which is useful for polemics and propaganda but less useful if you're trying to find out what happened. After looking into the evidence of the JFK assassination, reading the Warren Report and dozens of books, speaking to the police officer who was handcuffed to Lee Harvey Oswald when he was shot, as well as people who knew Jack Ruby (Oswald's assassin), I draw the conclusion that Oswald didn't shoot the President. That doesn't mean I also believe that he was killed by aliens, and it is pure confusion to connect the two.

On the other hand, it is true that sometimes when a person believes in one "conspiracy," that leads to believing in other "conspiracies." So why would that be? One good reason is that since no one learns conspiracies growing up or going to school in ordinary institutional settings, a person who discovers government malfeasance is more prone to examine other beliefs. In the same way that someone who - for example - grows up a fundamentalist Christian, only to later find out that the Bible contradicts itself at various points, may endure a crisis of faith. That person may find themselves reexamining their entire life and relationships.

Negative Evidence

Shermer says that since we can obtain a paper trail for some actual events, we should be able to obtain a paper trail for all conspiracies. It should be pretty easy to see what is wrong with Shermer's statement, since he assumes that all events are created equal, and all have the same sort of discoverable paper trail. Unfortunately, we know this isn't true. Just to take one example, the reason we have only limited information into the CIA's decades-long experimentation with human mind control is **that CIA Director Richard Helms ordered much of it destroyed.** We know this is true because Helm admitted doing it in congressional hearings in 1973. For another, there are thousands of records still unreleased pertaining to the Kennedy assassination, which keep getting set for release and then delayed, even by Donald Trump, whom some folks unwisely thought would be happy to release.

Notice something else about the three concepts put forward in the article. There are no positive facts or evidence submitted in the argumentation. They are all essentially handwaving responses. There is no effort to submit any evidence and no attempt to demarcate a **real conspiracy**, in their formulation - like the Reagan arms-for-hostages trade - and a **conspiracy theory**, such as Lee Harvey Oswald not killing JFK. Which of course brings back the essential fuzziness, the sponginess, of the concept itself.

The truth is that - as I have stated elsewhere - conspiracy theory is simply political analysis that the State doesn't like. Which brings us to the next point.

The State

What is missing from almost all analysis of conspiracies is the State. **The State is not value-free**. It is not objective. It is not a white background for the ink of history to write on. It is an aggressive and active participant in events. It has a point of view which is not monolithic with respect to every detail, but there is large general agreement about certain points.

In the United States at present, there are two major political parties, the Democrats and the Republicans. We also have a first-past-the-post or Winner Take All political system, which ensures that only one of these two parties maintains power at any given time. (Every other democracy on Earth has some form of parliamentary system, in which power can be apportioned to several parties, meaning that some cooperation is required.) The average U.S. citizen believes that there are enormous differences between the parties and often believe people who subscribe to the other party are treasonous.

Of course, in the main, the most striking thing about the Democrats and the Republicans is the wide *agreement* between them. The few differences between them are emphasized in the media and typically revolve around social issues. The dichotomy of Republican and Democrat enables certain questions to never be asked. Let's look at a few examples.

1. The United States has the right to interfere in other countries to pursue its national interest. Politicians might disagree about particular invasions or wars - or about the level of governance required for a particular invasion or war - or whether mercenaries should be used - *but our right to invade is **never** questioned*. When the public unrest was happening in Ferguson, Missouri, did it ever cross your mind that Vietnam

might send in troops to protect their interest? How about UN peacekeepers? Suppose Russia had decided that the unrest there might affect its investments and therefore it needed to invade to protect its investment. How would you feel about that?

2. Massive surveillance is required. The arguments tend to be whether Silicon Valley should be in charge or various governmental programs, but the political parties agree that it should be done.

3. Whistleblowers like Julian Assange should be prosecuted to the fullest extent of the law. Barack Obama, ostensibly a liberal, had a terrible record with whistleblowers - beginning right from 2009, the DOJ began prosecuting them under the Espionage Act. Speaking of Obama, it should be noted that although he ran on a platform of shutting down Guantanamo Bay, this did not happen. This supposed to be a key difference between Republicans and Democrats. In practice, not so much.

4. Israel should be supported with money and arms. The arguments are always about how much and how long, if there are arguments, but never about *whether we should*. That particular discussion just never happens in the mainstream. I am not saying that we shouldn't – in fact, the issue is extremely complex. However, one reason for popular dislike for American support for Israel is that most Americans are entirely ignorant of the history of

the region or why it is geopolitically important. However, no rational conversation on the issue can be had, and this extends to both parties.

There is also a marriage between elements of the media, government, and governmental-linked corporations such as Raytheon or Halliburton. A classic recent example: On June 21, 2019, the Washington Post ran an op-ed entitled "To avoid a wider war, Iran must be deterred with limited U.S. military strikes." It was written by Michael G. Vickers. Mr. Vickers joined the board of directors of BAE Systems in 2015, a company which makes attack drones for use by the U.S. military for war. The op-ed was therefore essentially an advertisement, run in a paper that most researchers know to be the CIA paper of record.

Without taking the State seriously as a positive actor, it becomes possible to filter everything for consumption by the public. Watergate is put forward, hilariously, as proof of the success of the system at preventing real conspiracies! Iran-Contra becomes further evidence of the self-correcting brilliance of the American political system. So that the lack of acceptance of government involvement in the Kennedy assassination proves that it is a baseless conspiracy theory, and the acceptance of government involvement in arms-for-hostages proves how great we are. The United States is the ultimate self-cleaning oven when it comes to corruption.

QAnon

The same thing applies to QAnon. QAnon folks do believe things that are inherently absurd, such as the idea that JFK Jr. is still alive and helping Donald Trump drain the swamp. But QAnon is not the fault of "conspiracy theorists." QAnon results from the State treating the American people like idiots for decades. **The lies perpetuated by the state have gotten so out of hand, and the public has so little say about public affairs, that they have been deceived by fraudsters out to make a buck. From the point of view of the State, the real problem with QAnon is that they are a competitor for dollars and attention.** Meanwhile, QAnon folks are not wrong about being screwed over. They are just under-educated and deliberately manipulated by unscrupulous people.

Generally, the media-governmental complex is engaged in a program to roll everybody into the category of conspiracy theorists. They deliberately conflate people who believe Donald Trump is exposing the elite pedophile network while the Democrats are using a voting system invented by Hugo Chavez to steal the election. Now this serves several purposes, but to begin with, it creates doubt about all such inquiries. **Because, by the way, there *is* a problem with institutional pedophilia.** One of the amazing things about the film *Spotlight*, which won a bunch of Oscars, is how blunt it is. Despite the critical response it received, the film seemed to recede under the waters and is rarely acknowledged now. I am going to take a minute here to go into the details of the film, because it's worth exploring, as the material shows that it is no longer tenable to assert that there are not large-scale conspiracies afoot in the world of business, government, law, and the Catholic Church. To argue otherwise is to both give moral support to those who would collude for the purposes of power and to submit to another's arbitrary authority.

Spotlight, directed by Tom McCarthy and based on the Boston Globe's extensive investigation into pedophilic priests, is one of the most important films of its kind ever made. One of the reasons the film works so well is because it proceeds – as a real investigation should – from a series of small details that lead to a larger context, which in this case implicates the Vatican itself.

The film begins by introducing us to the members of the Spotlight team, led by Walter Robinson (Keaton, beautifully understated), Mike Rezendes (Ruffalo), Sasha Pfieffer (MacAdams), and Matt Carroll (James), a group within the Globe whose job it is to perform long-term investigations. When the venerable newspaper hires its first Jewish editor, Marty Baron (Schreiber), he decides the first order of business is to pursue the local story of a priest accused of molesting young boys. This does not make the established order of Boston very happy. As the film explains, the Irish cops don't like to make the (clerical) collar; the judges don't want to make them testify; and the people don't like the threat to their own sense of community. Nobody wants to put God on trial.

What makes the film special is that it doesn't stop at the first priest, or even the tenth. In a scene that makes up the core of the picture, Marty Baron says the story is the "system." That is, the problem is systemic and they have the story only when they can indict the entire underlying structure that protects these pedophiles. And that particular angle does go all the way to the top – to the highest members of the clergy, and ultimately to the Vatican, which maneuvers these men from one parish to another, leaving a trail of victims. How did they hide the crimes? Through cash settlements. As depicted in *Spotlight*, the Holy Church used lawyers to arrange the payoffs.

The book *Betrayal: The Crisis in the Catholic Church*, by the investigative staff of the Boston Globe, goes into more detail: "In fact virtually all those who went to the Church with claims of sexual misconduct by priests received settlements before they filed suit, an arrangement that left no public record of the crime committed by the abusing priests."[iii]

One thing that struck me in both seeing the picture and reading the account afterward in *Betrayal*, is that at the beginning of the investigation the reporters were all in the position of conspiracy theorists. The more they probed the story, the more they had information implicating one of the most powerful and oldest institutions in the world in horrible crimes. They learned of networks, of backroom deals and of forces capable of altering court documents and destroying unwanted information. One of the fears in the movie, expressed by the Baron character, is that the Church would want to apologize and investigate its own messes. This is, in fact, exactly what it tried to do in the wake of the Globe's reporting.

After the initial Globe reports, the cardinal held a televised press conference at which he apologized for his past mistakes and promised to report any future allegations against priests to the authorities. As the Boston Globe reporters note: "He was basically saying, 'Trust us, give us the benefit of the doubt, we'll create a commission to make sure this doesn't happen again.' Well, we tried that. It didn't work."[iv]

The Church created 'treatment facilities' in which they would ship repeat offenders, but it turned out those facilities made essentially no real attempt to block access from the priests to the kids. So naturally the priests would repeat again.

We know, in fact, that no institution can police itself honestly that way. As we have seen over and over again with police departments, the CIA, and other governmental investigations, the mantra "we have investigated ourselves and found nothing wrong," is a recipe for corruption. It proved true in the Warren Commission, which came to an absurd conclusion in the Kennedy assassination, and it has failed again and again to find evidence of high crimes in public scandals.

"No institution can police itself," said David Clohessy, national director of the Survivors Network of those Abused by Priests. "If the Church wants to restore trust, leaders should be more open about these treatment facilities. If chemical companies said, 'Just trust us – send us your dioxins; we'll clean them up,' – the public would be wary."[v]

By dealing with its subject honestly and at least making an effort to expose the incredible scope of the Catholic Church's abuse scandal, *Spotlight* deserves immense credit. An absorbing, fascinating film, sharply made and efficient, it packs a punch. It earns its comparisons to *All the President's Men*, and if it isn't quite as slickly made, it has the benefit that the story it tells isn't a fairy tale designed to protect the CIA but a true indictment of established power. After all, what entity owns more land than the Vatican? Why does the Pope have a Swiss guard? Why are priests made to be celibate? (It has nothing to do with morality - it was to prevent priests from having heirs who might fight for property rights.) The more one scratches the surface of the Holy Mother Church, the more one finds a den of thieves who have turned the musings of a carpenter's son into a golden empire. In the 21st century, in a time when young people especially have started to understand the legacy of colonialism, the legacy of Catholicism cannot be ignored.

ON THE OTHER HAND

So there is strong evidence for an elite pedophile network in at least one area. Does that evidence extend to others? Yes and no. One problem has been that some people have allowed their conclusions in one arena to enable sweeping statements about all other arenas. You can't do that. You have to investigate these things the way archaeologists unearth dinosaur bones – one tiny dig at a time.

Unfortunately, with QAnon muddying the waters by insisting everyone in Hollywood is a pedophile without evidence, this creates doubt about a subject that no one really wants to investigate because of how nasty it is. Which means people write it off.

And this matches everything else we see in other topics. Leadership changes but nothing institutional really changes. For example, Nancy Pelosi declared her support for a bill that helps no one but multinational corporations and vaccine makers because Trump is out of the picture. The same thing is true of other "real" stories. Are there problems with voting machines? Absolutely. And you can read about some of those in Mark Crispin Miller, Greg Palast, and Stacey Abrams.

But there is a strict binary about what counts as a conspiracy theory. Let's say that I think Vladimir Putin murdered some of his rivals: *not conspiracy*. If I think that the Russians hacked the election, *not conspiracy*. If I think that there might be some bipedal mammals, very tall and heavy, living in forest and swamp areas, which have been observed thousands of times anecdotally and by some indigenous peoples: *conspiracy theory.*

Which is not to say I have a dog in the argument about Bigfoot. I just don't think it's a ridiculous enterprise. It's certainly no more ridiculous than physicists who insist there are multiple universes, which is one of the dumbest ideas to ever get wide promulgation. And yet perfectly acceptable to mention at a dinner party.

The larger point that I'm trying to make is that **conspiracy theory isn't a special type of claim**. It's an observation about the world that uses the same toolkit a scientist or a logician does. You investigate things the best you can and recognize that there are strong points and weak points and you make sense of the world. It's not like people are born conspiracy theorists. They are made. They are made by circumstance.

So in all this is a serious point. Being able to successfully identify conspiracies is exactly what you need to be able to do in order to track all the illegal stuff they are inevitably trying to get away with. So the State will smear any parapolitical researcher with being a member of a dangerous club, or equate them with QAnon. Because people who are able to track them are a threat to their existence. At the moment there is an increasing consolidation of the internet to turn it into something that any Chinese bureaucrat would love, based on the alleged danger of people saying mean things. Anyone who is investigating anything that is "fringe" should have a vested interest in this process. It's too important to just let it be under the control of either corrupt statists or technocratic utopians.

"You understand what I'm saying? We knew we couldn't make it illegal to be either against the war or black, but by getting the public to associate the hippies with marijuana and blacks with heroin, and then criminalizing both heavily, we could disrupt those communities...We could arrest their leaders. raid their homes, break up their meetings, and vilify them night after night on the evening news. Did we know we were lying about the drugs? Of course we did."

-Richard Nixon's former counsel John Ehrlichman, from an interview in Harper's Magazine that wasn't printed *until 22 years after* it was completed

ON THE ORIGINS OF SEDITIOUS DISCOURSE

"The first concern of any dictatorship is, consequently, to subjugate both labor and culture...in my opinion, there are two ways for an intellectual to betray at present, and in both cases he betrays because he accepts a single thing - that separation between labor and culture. The first way is characteristic of bourgeois intellectuals who are willing that their privileges should be paid for by the enslavement of the workers. They often say they are defending freedom, but they are defending first of all the privileges freedom gives to them, and to them alone. **The second way is characteristic of intellectuals who think they are leftist and who, through distrust of freedom, are willing that culture, and the freedom it presupposes, should be directed, under the vain pretext of serving a future justice.**"

- Albert Camus, *Resistance, Rebellion, and Death* (95; emphasis mine.)

We are, as ever, cursed to live in interesting times. One interesting thing is that as a society we have grown to recognize an enormous variety of sexual and gender expressions in human beings, while reaffirming that political expression can only be filtered and understood via a binary of opposites. That is, while I can identify as trans, or as a furry, or look forward to a future in which I can marry a sex doll, I am limited for all practical purposes to identifying as a Democrat or a Republican. Only the left wing or the right wing of that Roman eagle will do.

Incidentally, these identities are defined in the most doctrinaire way, so that Bernie Sanders is not an appropriate Democrat (too *Socialist*) and is therefore a man without a party. At the same time, the Republican party is split up into more or less traditional conservatives and Trump Republicans, whose beliefs are subject to the chaotic whims of their chosen man. Liberal Democrats (and liberals in general) have become extremely reactionary and conservative in defining the boundaries of who is allowed in the debate and what the terms of the debate must be. Republicans, for their part, have become liberalized into somehow making obvious criminality and sexual aggression the traits of a perfect godly leader, which is logical pandemonium even for fundamentalists.

At the same time, all the discussion about politics in this country on major media – whether on National Public Radio or Fox News – surprise not with their polarization but with their fundamental *agreement* on a set of myths which all sensible Americans are engaged to support. So, for example, the question is what measures are allowed in defense of global terrorism – not how terrorists should be defined or whether they are an outcome of our own foreign policy. A typical issue that arises is: *How far should the National Security State be allowed to go in order to spy on Americans?* Rather than, *why do we have this apparatus and whom does it serve? Should we dismantle it? Why should we pay for it, rather than, say, healthcare or infrastructure?*

In order to participate in the political arena, we must also accept that a lone nut killed Lee Harvey Oswald, that James Earl Ray killed Dr. King, that Sirhan Sirhan remains rightly confined for murdering RFK, that the Black Panthers were dangerous radicals that deserved to be exterminated and/or imprisoned, that Osama bin Laden perpetrated 9/11, that there was nothing suspicious about the subsequent mailing of anthrax to prominent Democrats opposed to the Patriot Act, and a hundred other things that are manifestly false. No wonder people hate talking politics. Even if they are unfamiliar with the details, they sense the lies underlying the positions of both parties and grow disgusted with their representatives.

Unfortunately, people often stop there and pick a party, deciding that the other party must be the problem, and dig their heels in. The other side is either stupid or misled or, in some formulations, a blot on society – that becomes the mantra.

This type of thinking leads to some truly inane ideas becoming common currency. At the present, the media continues to be obsessed with this notion that Russians hacked the election. The peculiar obsession has neatly flipped the typical narrative of right-wing Republicans being anti-Communist and anti-Russia, whereas now the Left rattles sabers and warns of Russian influence practically every evening on MSNBC.

Secondarily, as a result of all this commotion, the language of conspiracy is everywhere. However, these are Ukrainian and Russian conspiracies – one primarily promulgated by the Left (against Trump) and one by the Right (against Biden and his son, hardly relevant figures at this point). So it seems to validate Ishmael Reed's remark in his novel *Mumbo Jumbo* that the world consists of "competing conspiracies." Indeed it does, although as far as the major media is concerned, only the conspiracies *they choose* to be important are important. Epstein, the various political assassinations, 9/11, these are all still mere "conspiracy theory" and therefore off limits. However, that the Russians gave Trump the election through purchasing ads on Facebook is just good reporting.

F. A. Hayek, in his short article "The Primacy of the Abstract," written as part of the 1968 Alpbach Symposium, observed that abstraction comes before concrete particulars in the human brain; that is, our ability to abstract is innate and comes *a priori*, before observation. In other words, we can't see an elephant until we have sufficient understanding of spatial relationships to construct a picture in our brain of where the elephant ends and the rest of the world begins.[vi] This is a possibly useful metaphor for what I am about to do, which is to cover some historical examples of controversies between the State and seditious thinking – i.e., ideas that the State doesn't like. For a first example, it is perfectly possible to understand why the Romans would have crucified Jesus even if you take all the metaphysical part of it out of the story. Jesus was proclaiming ideas – healing the sick, taking care of those less fortunate, caring about the general populace rather than investment income – which were inimical to the Roman state. The Romans would have quite rightly assessed that if Jesus became popular, this would not be good for them. Hence crucifixion. Jesus and the Roman state assessed the concrete particulars of their situation the same way; they merely differed about the primary abstraction, which is to say the lens used to view those particulars.

OK, so given this context, the question remains: What the hell is going on?

On the one hand, some of this is business as usual. The origins of the arguments about free speech and Fake News can be traced back to at least Martin Luther. One of the major complaints about the old Catholic church was its insistence in using Latin for church services for the laity. Since most parishioners were uneducated, they did not understand the actual words that they were being expected to hold sacred. Martin Luther, for his part, was not anti-Latin; actually, he thought it important for people to be educated in that language – but he also found other languages acceptable for church service. In the *Deutsche Messe* of 1526 he wrote: "I do not ... wish to eliminate or change it [the Latin language], but rather, as we have preserved it among us until now, so should it remain free to employ it, where and when it pleases us or reasons compel us. I do not wish to give them any means to allow the Latin language to leave the worship service entirely, for I must do everything for the sake of youth." He was not as radical as some of his fellows in wanting to eliminate Latin, but he did think it was important to be able to disseminate the Word in other tongues. But Martin Luther had more faith in the Word than did the Catholic hierarchy, for the Church's interests have always been in power and real estate. At various times, some of its own intellectual and philosophical members had produced cognitive arguments, for example, against the existence of God. And so within the Church there were healthy correspondences about the Ontological argument and so on, along with a fair amount of nonsense. This is the price one pays for even a limited amount of free speech.

Even where there was no physical injury (that is, torture or being burnt at the stake), there remained social controls. For example, when the German philosopher Leibniz died in 1716, an entire system of thought (*The Monadology*) was discovered in his desk. The inventor of the calculus, Leibniz had promulgated a ridiculous philosophy during his life (that this is the best of all possible worlds, rightly satirized by Voltaire in his hilarious novel *Candide*) and left his most complex creation to be discovered after his death.

The reason I bring all of this up is because it is often remarked that we live in a special time, begun by the election of Donald Trump to high office. It is in one sense, which Kenn Thomas incisively observed in his book *Trumpocalypse Now* as the "triumph of the conspiracy spectacle," but it is also largely false in that he is a wild card in a long chain of historical events. There have been repeated patterns of coercion and freedom struggling against one another throughout all history. The State seeks to limit thought, and certain individuals seek to release it. And conspiracy theories have frequently been at the center of this war. Neil Postman provides one early example:

> ...by the late seventeenth century, there was a beginning to a native literature that turned out to have as much to do with the typographic bias of American culture as books. I refer, of course, to the newspaper, at which Americans first tried their hands on September 25, 1690, in Boston, when Benjamin Harris printed the first edition of a three-page paper he called *Publick Occurrences Both Foreign and Domestick*. Before he came to America, Harris had played a role in 'exposing' a nonexistent conspiracy of Catholics to slaughter Protestants and burn London...He

concluded his prospectus with the following sentence: 'It is suppos'd that none will dislike this Proposal but such as intend to be guilty of the crime.' Harris was right about who would dislike his proposal...The Governor and Council suppressed it, complaining that Harris had printed 'reflections of a very high nature,' by which they meant they had no intention of admitting any impediments to whatever villainy they wished to pursue.[vii]

Now Postman is obviously not endorsing this conspiracy, nor is he saying that the Governor and Council suppressed it because they were in on it. Probably they didn't believe the story or take it seriously. (Although frankly, looking at the history of the Catholic church, it's less far-fetched than it might seem on the surface.)

But they suppressed it anyway.

And *that's* the point.

In the somewhat hagiographic documentary about Noam Chomsky, *Manufacturing Consent*, the episode involving Robert Faurisson is covered in some detail. Faurisson is a Holocaust denier, but he had also written some other things of some historical value to some academics. In any case, the publisher asked Chomsky to provide an introduction about free speech. Chomsky did so, and the resulting brouhaha forced him into the position of defending himself against charges of endorsing Holocaust denial. Chomsky is very clear: He does not endorse the ideas. He endorses Faurisson's right to pursue the ideas. And he says another simple clear statement: "Either you are for free speech you don't like, or you are not for free speech."

This is exactly correct. And I am not one to endorse Chomsky, but credit where credit is due. Do I think anyone who denies the Holocaust occurred has a leg to stand on? No. Do I think they should be allowed to do research and publish their work? Of course. If you don't believe that, you are not for free speech and are aligning yourself with the State.

I have argued in another essay ("Why the State Hates Conspiracy" in *Deep Truth Journal*) that understanding conspiracy theories – the real ones – requires enormous work that the State will never endorse or assist. In fact, they will deny their very existence unless forced to acknowledge them. J. Edgar Hoover used to tell people the Mafia was a "myth." A conspiracy theory. Why? Because it was easier for him to do his work if people thought this was so – and also because he liked betting the horses and got good tips from Frank Costello.[viii]

Incidentally, these conspiracies and secret teams that infest our own political processes have always been around. Douglas Rushkoff explicitly makes the point like so:

In the Middle Ages, the coercive power of architecture was so well appreciated, in fact, that builders formed secret societies dedicated to keeping these technologies for themselves. Very few people understood how a vaulted arch was actually constructed, or why it defied gravity. Architects and the institutions they served maintained their authority by keeping this information guarded – the same way technology companies protect hi-tech secrets today.[ix]

Rushkoff is dead-on here. There is nothing new under the sun when it comes to secret societies, conspiracies, and a powerful minority exercising control over a majority which performs its labor.

WWI AND WW2

This type of thinking can manipulate the people into getting into a war. It happened during World War I. Why would the United States join the battle? The primary dispute was between the Slavic portions of Hungary (including Bosnia) which desired independence. The Archduke Franz Ferdinand was in favor of independence, at least after a fashion (his plan included a tripartite union of independent states). He was assassinated by a Serb who disagreed. Thus began a domino effect in which nation after nation entered into war, squabbling about their specific 'possessions' with one another.

One thing that was present in the European countries was the memory of old wounds, together with feelings that every other country was trying to take over the world. For example, many French wanted revenge for their defeat in 1870 by the Germans, and harbored general anti-German feeling. Many Brits felt that Germany wanted to destroy the British Empire, and thus considered war as a form of self-defense. Americans did not share these feelings.

Generally speaking, Americans (apart from Teddy Roosevelt) did not want to participate in the war until the pivotal sinking of the Lusitania. But even then there were many pieces published urging judicious reflection. However, the *business populace* was geared up for war and seized on the opportunity. It is a fact that America did a great deal more business with England and France than it did with Germany. It is another fact that American business with the former two countries exploded during WWI. As Barbara Tuchman writes in her seminal history of the period: "Trade with the Central Powers declined from $169 million to $1 million in 1916, and during the same period trade with the Allies rose from $824 million to $3 billion...Eventually, the United States became the larder, arsenal, and bank of the Allies and acquired a direct interest in Allied victory that was to bemuse the postwar apostles of economic determinism for a long time."[x]

EDWARD BERNAYS

After World War II, with the United States taking the primary position as beacon of Western civilization, the propaganda necessary to keep the populace at bay grew more sophisticated. The nostalgia that many baby boomers feel about the Fifties is colored by news and television ads promising a better America and an air of progressive education. It was also colored by a man called Edward Bernays.

I.G. Farben, one of the worst offenders among those companies doing business with Hitler, hired Edward Bernays to provide spin control. He is often described as the father of public relations.

By the mid 1920's, Bernays had gotten a foothold among large corporate clients in need of spin control. The nephew of Sigmund Freud, he had been working in his invented field for about ten years, but which only now began paying large dividends. He wrote books with titles such as *Propaganda* and *The Engineering of Consent.* Among his many 'accomplishments' was inventing the hearty breakfast: "He helped jump-start sales of bacon, a breakfast rarity until the 1920s, by enlisting a prominent doctor to solicit fellow doctors' opinions on the salutary benefits of a hearty breakfast and by arranging to have famous figures photographed eating breakfasts of bacon and eggs."[xi] Bernays was thus the inventor of those television commercials that purport to tell us that '4 out of 5 doctors' agree that Product X is superior to Product Y.

Bernays clients, in 1929, boasted a lineup of powerful corporations: New Jersey Bell, Procter & Gamble, Knox Gelatin, and American Tobacco. He also pulled off an absurd P.R. blitz by General Electric this year, at a time when G.E. was experiencing some image issues. He had G.E. sponsor an event in praise of Thomas Edison's invention of the light bulb.

Edison was not particularly inclined to help G.E. In 1891, J. P. Morgan had wrested away the Edison General Electric Company from the famed inventor of the light bulb. As soon as his feat was accomplished, Morgan removed Edison's name from the company and rechristened it General Electric. (G. E., of course, went on to become one of the most powerful corporations in the United States, eventually owning – among other holdings – the National Broadcasting Company, NBC.) Still, Edison ended up going along with it, despite his decided ambivalence toward General Electric.[xii]

Bernays also found his way, as one might imagine, to helping the tobacco industry, creating what may have been the first 'front group.' A now-common strategy used by industries, a 'front group' is a paid-for 'grassroots' lobby group that supports whatever those in power want. So, for example, the CIA uses the False Memory Syndrome Foundation, a front group that lends its voice to television networks and *Skeptic* magazine, to try and drown out people who claim to have had memories traumatically erased. These front groups then become the primary voice to the media outlets, and shout down any attempt to produce evidence or facts in contradiction to their chosen cause.

REFORM

The right-wing elements in this country have always aligned themselves with the State. It's their bread and butter. God and bullets, along with freedom for petrochemical and munitions companies. However, what seems to have happened now is that Trump has provided a way for these same forces to co-opt what would otherwise be the left.

Whether the issue is climate change, or gun control, or children's education – all obviously important topics – many on the left are ceding intellectual space to State forces. They are demanding that corporations not only police themselves but police ourselves. *Which is happening.* So YouTube has announced that it is changing its algorithms to prevent people from reaching "borderline" content. Who determines what constitutes borderline content? Nobody knows, but they are looking at "...stuff that toes the line of its acceptable content policies. In practice this means stuff like videos that make nonsense claims the earth is flat, or blatant lies about historical events such as the 9/11 terror attacks, or promote harmful junk about bogus miracle cures for serious illnesses."[xiii]

It's easy to coat efforts by YouTube and Google or Amazon as civic responsibility – *just think of the children!* But it's obvious that these definitions are always going to be modeled on what the State wants, when what the State wants is a quiet marketplace for big businesses to continue providing economic power for the State. It's already happened in other parts of the language – for example, "economic freedom" means the opposite of what is normally meant by "freedom." And cheerleaders like Thomas Friedman make no bones about it: "In the workshops devoted to creating the indexes, Friedman cited the example of Hong Kong as evidence for the truth of this proposition, saying: "There is almost no doubt that if you had political freedom in Hong Kong you would have much less economic and civil freedom than you do as a result of an authoritarian government.""[xiv] Greg Palast notes that he "was there" at the University of Chicago when this economic revolution in language happened, and spells it out in great detail in his excellent book *The Best Democracy Money Can Buy.*[xv] It's informed by his experiences at Ground Zero of the economic "miracle" that is currently destroying all of our lives as we scramble around trying to make a living wage in a service economy.

A recent story done by Yahoo finance is a perfect example of this continued fight. The story, titled *The internet 'is at a real crossroads,' World Wide Web Foundation CEO warns*, by Kristen Despotakis, contains a long quote by World Wide Web Foundation CEO Adrian Lovett. It goes as follows:

"I think the place we're at right now is at a real crossroads...On the one hand, we can see an incredibly exciting path for the World Wide Web [that] is nurturing, that is creative, that is liberating, that enables people to build businesses to claim their basic rights, all of the very best of the web that we've seen over the past 25 years or so."

"But there's another path that we are all more than familiar with," he continued, "which is a much more dystopian, dark path where we have increasing numbers of data breaches, the further spread of disinformation and misinformation, further action by governments to shut down [internet access] in different parts of the world — parts of the web, and to censor it. So all of those things add up to, we think, a moment of opportunity."[xvi]

Note: The *liberating* path is the one which is great for *business*. The *dystopian* path is the one dominated by misinformation and disinformation, which is of course based on the State's point of view. We agree on the particulars but not the abstraction. Sure, this is high tech, but we might as well be back in 1690 regarding the relationships.

If you give the likes of Mark Zuckerberg the write to determine free speech, you won't have free speech. And if you don't have free speech, you are helpless against the State. Right now the left is so obsessed with reenacting *The Crucible* on Twitter that they don't see that they aren't the witches — they're the hysterics pointing at all the witches. I'm not saying Trump isn't awful. I'm saying that if history has taught us anything, Pete "CIA" Buttegieg is not the answer.

Are there villains in politics? You bet. Are they uniformly Russian agents? Of course not. The world is much too complicated to have only one tool in your toolkit. Freedom — actual freedom — the freedom to think thoughts, to express thoughts, and to engage in collective action — matters far more than the "economic freedom" desired by corporations who wish to possess the means to hoard and sell water to parched citizens. History has given us the context to understand what I believe will be the central conflict of the rest of the century.

"Behind the ostensible government sits enthroned an invisible government owing no allegiance and acknowledging no responsibility to the people. To destroy this invisible government, to befoul the unholy alliance between corrupt business and corrupt politics is the first task of the statesmanship of the day."

    -Teddy Roosevelt, 1906

"The new economy will, as we have seen, be no state or governmental economy but a private economy committed to a civic power of resolution which certainly will require state cooperation for organic consolidation to overcome inner friction and increase production and endurance."

-Walter Rathenau, *The New Political Economy*

72

WHY THE STATE HATES CONSPIRACY

L. Frank Baum, famous now for being the author of the *Wizard of Oz* books, was not well known in his day for his writings. He was better known for his talent at creating fantasy, as a designer of department stores. His job was to envision a place where consumers could realize all of their dreams in a magical land and he was quite successful at it. There aren't many department stores now, but when they first appeared on the American scene it was a bit like changing the world from grey to Technicolor: Every want, every need, satisfied on every floor, an assemblage of wonders to engage every sense. In other words, Baum was doing for capitalism what the Wizard was doing for the kingdom.

However, pay no attention to that man behind the curtain.

The United States has long been a place obsessed with symbols, many of them adopted from empires past – the flag, the eagle, the torch, the obelisk. Those symbols, together with some help from propagandistic historians, Hollywood, and a deliberately stunted educational system, have covered over the fact that the U.S. has operated like most bureaucratic governments do in expanding as far and as fast as possible. And it all works, as long as you accept the Wizard and never look behind the curtain.

Which is why the state hates conspiracy.

WHAT COUNTS AS A CONSPIRACY?

On August 17, 2016, the London Guardian newspaper, not known for tabloid tendencies, ran a story about a ritual human sacrifice being filmed at CERN. Located in Geneva, CERN is the European Organization for Nuclear Research. It serves as the home of the Large Hadron Collider and the now – decommissioned Synchro –Cyclotron, and other devices designed to poke forcefully into the nature of reality. For these reasons alone it is the focus of much speculation, but the designers of the facility also placed a large statue of Shiva the Destroyer in front of the entrance. Why they did this is anyone's guess.

So there's already a portentous Lovecraftian aura to the place even before you get to the ritual snuff flick. In the video, we see several black-cloaked men emerge out of the darkness, prepare a woman who lies down in

74

front of Shiva, before she is stabbed. The cameraman, filming from high above inside the main building at CERN, gives a start and begins running – a nice dramatic touch. A spokeswoman for CERN noted two things of interest: CERN's disapproval of such shenanigans, which causes "...misunderstandings about the scientific nature of our work," and the confirmation that the participants had access badges. Both the spokeswoman and the Guardian treat the incident as a harmless prank.[xvii]

The idea that the incident was a mock ritual human sacrifice rather than an actual ritual human sacrifice is to be preferred, certainly; and yet this doesn't seem particularly comforting. Scientists (or assistants, or in any case people entrusted with going in and out of the building with the most powerful particle accelerators in the world) decided to perform a ritual with echoes of *Eyes Wide Shut* in front of a pagan statue. No explanation is forthcoming; although the incident makes it into the papers, it is resolved by a public relations person and sent to bed.

I refer to incidents like this as The Weirdness. Every now and then The Weirdness pokes through in the major media. As with this fake human sacrifice, the story fades away and is replaced by the normal shuffle of news, consisting of Latin American coups, fat-shaming opinion pieces, and actresses informing us all how much fun they had on the set. There could be a million reasons why the major media pursues certain stories doggedly and leaves others with barely a sniff, but for now let's just be aware that it happens. *Someone*, presumably the media, picks and chooses what gets emphasized, and repeated, and pounded into the national consciousness.

One might observe that this is less true than it used to be, thanks to the Internet, but only slightly so. The fact is that many alternative sources of news are partly or wholly derivative of the main news organizations. Aggregator websites like *What Really Happened*, for example, often pronounce the death of the major media while being *almost entirely dependent on it for all content*. Other news sources have made some inroads and carved out their own niches, but when it comes to big stories they cannot compete with the production behemoths of the alphabet networks. With the recent removal of Net Neutrality, the future looks to be ever more controlled.

So how does the media choose their stories? And, perhaps more importantly, how do they present them? Because even when stories are presented that have a "weird" or conspiratorial aspect, they are presented with scare quotes. The exception to this is when the conspiracy involves another country or otherwise does not implicate the U.S. government. For example:

On January 21, 2016, it was reported that Vladimir Putin, the Russian Prime Minister, gave approval for the murder of a former Russian spy, Alexander Litvinenko. Mr. Litvinenko had been poisoned in 2006. The Russian Foreign Ministry disagreed and complained that politics, not evidence, played a role in the accusation.

Major media, including the BBC, New York Post, and other outlets reported the story. Putin, the ruthless former head of the KGB, killed a Russian spy.

Conspiracy theory? No.

Let's take a different example.

On March 30, 1981, a young man named John Hinckley, Jr., attempted to assassinate President Ronald Reagan. He apparently shot Reagan, along with James Brady and others. Hinckley was apprehended.

Hinckley came from an oil background, and his family and the family of George Bush, then-Vice President, were intimate friends. It turned out that Neil Bush was going to have dinner with Hinckley's brother a night after the shooting.
The ties between Hinckley and Bush, the ruthless former head of the CIA, were never formally investigated.

Conspiracy theory? Yes.

What is the relevant difference between these two stories?

At the moment, the world is worked up because of an apparent "hacking" of the U.S. election that was allegedly perpetrated by the Russians, in league with Donald Trump. Pursuing the case is Robert Mueller, former Yale Skull and Bones (like John Kerry and George Bush), the FBI Director who also happens to be married to Ann Cabell Standish, the granddaughter of Charles Cabell. Charles Cabell was the former CIA Director who has fired by JFK after the Bay of Pigs disaster. His brother Earle Cabell was the mayor of Dallas when Kennedy was shot on November 22, 1963. Hackers who ran fake ads on Facebook, thus convincing people to vote for Donald Trump, launched this Russian conspiracy.

No issues there, right? Makes perfect sense. There were lots of people, in the lead up to the election, torn between voting for Hilary Clinton and Donald Trump. "Clinton, Trump...I wish there was something to help me decide. Oh wow, this ad says Hilary Clinton is a bad person. Well, that tears it." *Have you ever met a single person in your life that was weighing whether to vote for Clinton or Trump?*

Which is not to say that I don't think Trump isn't atrocious. I'm just pointing out that this is clearly a **conspiracy theory**, and even on its own terms *it makes no sense*. Which is also not to say it didn't happen; Trump and his son-in-law seem to be exactly the sorts of idiots who would get in bed with this scheme.

I'm just asking why I'm a thoughtful citizen if I believe in the Russian conspiracy, but a diseased lunatic if I believe in a JFK assassination conspiracy, when *there is a great deal more actual evidence for the latter.*

THE GOOD OLD DAYS

In the good old days of media monopoly, it was easy.

William Randolph Hearst was a great admirer of both Adolf Hitler and Italy's Benito Mussolini. So in 1934 he offered them both jobs writing in Hearst publications. At the time, Hearst was the most powerful newspaperman in America, having built and empire of yellow journalism across the nation. He was so well known that by 1941, Orson Welles would get in some hot water with his satirical film *Citizen Kane*, largely based on Hearst.

While Hitler declined the honor of writing columns, his propaganda minister Joseph Goebbels bought much positive coverage from Hearst for $400,000. For his part, Mussolini agreed to become a columnist; although a newspaperman himself, he had better things to do than actually write the columns, so he delegated it to one of his lovers. Thus the United Press wire began running columns written by Mussolini's mistress.

At the time, despite Hitler's having taken power in 1933 in Germany, the great fear among American industrialists and Hearst himself was communism. As Hearst biographer W. A. Swanburg put it:

> Doubtless Hearst saw in fascism a useful bulwark against Communism, which terrified him with its threat to liberty and private property. If he had to choose between the two, he would certainly have picked fascism, but the evidence indicates he preferred traditional American democracy above all.[xviii]

In our time, it's traditionally argued that it is more difficult to rule over the media – except for counterexamples like Rupert Murdoch. Indeed, Donald Trump has dominated a generally hostile media simply by not playing the normal rules of politics and being perpetually outrageous. Entertainment trumps reason, or so it seems. That is partly because the medium itself – television – depends on perpetuating interest in an audience, which often means simplification and hype in equal measure. This extends from right-wing talk shows on Fox to allegedly left- wing programs like The Daily Show. Trump is as good for one as the other.

The essence of drama is conflict. The simplest dramas involve the conflict of two clearly defined opposing forces. Man v Nature. Good v Evil. It's part of the reason comic books, and comic book movies, are so popular. Captain America v Iron Man. Batman v Superman. We are naturally attracted to dichotomy. It's the way sports is sold, too – Jordan v Bird, Kobe v Duncan, Peyton Manning v Tom Brady and so on. Politics is no different. One is either liberal or conservative, one watches Fox News or CNN, and so on. With the growth of the Internet, this is less true than it used to be; however, new dichotomies have replaced these as television slowly fades away. Science v Religion is a popular one. Feminists v Anti-Feminists. The arguments about safe spaces and the battles over language appear in many blogs and comment areas. In fact, virtually everything in the world is presented and accepted in terms of binaries in which one picks a side. *Us and Them*, like the Pink Floyd song goes.

If we are to try and get outside standard thinking we need to recognize that this style of presenting all ideas in terms of a binary structure is not inevitable. *It's a choice.* In many cases, the choice to present stark terms originates from advertising and storytelling. And there's nothing wrong with that per se, except that most real-world situations are much more complex. The reality is that any attempt to deconstruct human history will be enormously complex, and we need to understand that before we try.

POLITICS AND ORIGINS

Everything has an origin story, and if you want to find out why this present moment in America is obsessed with conspiracy theories, we have to go back to the Second World War.

When the United States government, led by President Roosevelt, decided to enter the fray in World War II and stop the Nazi threat, one consequence was that it was a boon for business. Wars are always good for business, and indeed many of great American fortunes began with wars of one kind or another. The ramping up of production, followed by victory in war, meant that the government was in a position to step back and make decisions about what the remaining half-century would look like from a position of dominance.

One of the immediate issues presented was whether to scale down the military in light of victory. Edwin Nourse, the chairman of President Harry Truman's Council of Economic Advisers (CEA) advocated using the resources developed for war to projects for the citizenry. No one could deny, however, that the war had exploded production in the United States, and powerful people lined up in opposition to Nourse: Dean Acheson, Leon Keyserling, George Kennan, and James Forrestal, among others. Acheson fired Nourse and replaced him with Keyserling. The days of the New Deal would be over, and the switch to militarist capitalism had been made.

...the U.S. business community, led by General Electric, not only was in favor of the bomb's use on Japan but collectively agreed on the 'necessity' of a permanent war economy for the postwar years. Reluctant to downscale industrial production to prewar levels, the corporate sector also perceived the lucrative benefits of continuing military contracts.

In January 1944 GE's [Charles]Wilson, vice--chair of the War Production Board...gave a speech to the Army Ordnance association in which he characterized disarmament as a 'thoroughly discredited doctrine' and advocated that the United States 'Should henceforth mount a national policy upon the solid fact of an industrial capacity for war, and a research capacity for war.' Many authorities point to this speech and the concepts Wilson advocated as the beginning of the postwar U.S. policy of an unprecedented military economy.[xix]

This was the tipping point in American history, except it leaves out one important detail. Even before the end of the War, Russian – not Germany – was largely seen as the ultimate threat. The fascists, in spite of their irrational exuberance, were still basically in favor of ruling the way we (and the British) prefer to rule. It was that damned communism that was the real problem. And at the end of the War, we imported not only Nazi scientists but also historians, as well as Reinhard Gehlen. Gehlen would be tapped as the most important "spy" into the Soviet territories we had, and his overestimations of Russian weaponry – and the eagerness of the Pentagon to hear his message – became an important part of the developing Cold War.

We co-opted the enemy, for fun and profit.

A LEARNED APPROACH

How does somebody become a conspiracy theorist? Are some people born conspiracy theorists? No, although all of us are born with pattern-recognition tendencies that might fail on us from time to time. In general, nonetheless, it is safe to say that few, if any children, are taught to be conspiracy theorists growing up.

How do children grow up in the United States? For the poor and working- class, the state has its way with them in public education. Public education was designed to teach children just enough to function in the 'modern' world – that is, the industrial society that was coming about at the same time pubic education became a state responsibility. Except for a tiny percentage of people in the patrician class, those who will be needed to fill elite jobs and make decisions for everyone else, public schooling is designed to generate middling adults – smart enough to handle the tasks of maintaining and cleaning up our civilization, but not so smart they grow unsatisfied with their burden.

As John Taylor Gatto observes, public education grew out of Prussia's loss to the French upstart Napoleon at the Battle of Jena. The type of schooling that Prussia initiated ended up being exported to the United States by, among others, Horace Mann.

> So the world got compulsion schooling at
> the end of a state bayonet for the first time
> in human history; modern forced schooling
> started in Prussia in 1819 with a clear vision

of what centralized schools could deliver:
1. Obedient soldiers to the army;
2. Obedient workers to the mines;
3. Well subordinated civil servant to government;
4. Well subordinated clerks to industry;
5. Citizens who thought alike about major issues.[xx]

The larger point is that the state has no interest in inculcating 'conspiracythinking' into the youth. For that matter, normal critical thinking tends to be pushed aside in favor of rote memory for the purpose of standardized testing. Classes are often overcrowded, and rarely more than an hour at a time before the bell rings, signaling all to move to the next class. Learning anything under these circumstances would be difficult, and indeed America's sliding rankings in the world bear this out.

Even if teachers wanted to add complexity to the understanding of, say, the war of 1812, the Lincoln assassination, or the Kennedy assassination, just to take a few examples, the entire enterprise of schooling itself mitigates against them.

So we have a question of ontology here: *How do conspiracy theorists become conspiracy theorists?*

The answer is *on their own.*

The child who is raised in a fundamentalist Christian household and becomes an atheist in adulthood does so fighting against all they've been taught. Somehow there was an inciting event – they learned some detail, often by happenstance, which set off their curiosity. Then they poked around and found whole new universes of information.

For myself, as a young child, I was an altar boy at St. Peter's, the barrio Catholic school I attended. Even as a child I questioned the stories of men in whales, resurrection, and feeding the multitudes with bread and two fish. What really did it for me, however, was a book that my father had around the house. He was a university history professor, and so had any number of academic books on the shelves. One of these was an archaeological survey of the Holy Land. In this book, it was found time and again that the sites visited had no connection to their Biblical description. *The Bible had mistakes in it.*

When I was eleven or twelve years old, I asked my parents for Bertrand Russell's book *Why I Am Not a Christian*. That, coupled with Pascal's *Pensees* and Plato's *Republic*, set me to studying philosophy for the better part of two decades.

BROTHER, CAN YOU PARADIGM?

The D.C. peace activist and Warren Commission critic John Judge coined a phrase to describe how he felt about standard ways of looking at the world: "Brother, can you paradigm?" A paradigm is a model for interpretation. We all use paradigms when we view the world; however, problems arise when paradigms get in the way of the truth – as can happen in science and academia.

In academia, university professors survive and obtain tenure is by acquiring a unique sandbox. That is, they find a particular specialty and become the expert in that specialty through long hours of dedicated study. (As Penn Jones used to say, "find some part of the case and research the hell out of it.") In some ways that is a good thing; the universe is a big place, with an infinite number of topics that cannot all be covered by a single person, so the piecemeal assignation that goes on is helpful toward a goal of general knowledge. When the AIDS epidemic first hit, many of the top scientists who ended up working in the field of AIDS had backgrounds in veterinary science. That's because the first cases involved cryptosporidium, a disease that had typically only been found in cattle up to that time. The morphology of the AIDS virus (that is to say, what it looked like) is similar to a sheep or cattle virus. In this case, having specialists who had experience in this area proved useful in another area, and this is the sort of the thing that happens all the time.

However, like the deliberate monotony of public school, the development of sandboxes – or paradigms – can also be something that inhibits knowledge. Once the sandbox is acquired, and a person's personal reputation, livelihood, and status is dependent on it, a person can be very reluctant to give it up. When Bertrand Russell was a teenager, he wrote a letter to the German logician Gottlieb Frege that destroyed his entire system of thought. Frege first denied it, then claimed that "the whole of mathematics is undermined." Which of course it wasn't. It's just that his theory was wrong. He never recovered from this, and we can have empathy for him while recognizing that sandboxes, and paradigms, can be as dangerous as they are helpful. The key, as in most things in life, is to remain flexible and adaptable.

There's one more aspect to this sandbox/paradigm concept. When a professor spends all or most of his or her time in that sandbox, the rest of his or her information about the world tends to stay frozen. They may retain some general knowledge about the rest of the world, but it becomes sketchier and less relevant over time. To their credit, they know this, which is why they rely on experts in their own sandboxes in discussions about areas not relevant to their own. And so everybody is an expert in one thing and vaguely cognizant of everything else.

That's point one. Point two is that there is a specific manner in which academic professors think that can best be captured, I think, with the term categorization. Everything about the university experience is categorized. *Art History 101. Brit Lit 1* and *2. American History* is often broken up from the revolution to the Civil War, then the Civil War to the present. And so on, in more and more specific detail. I am not arguing against this. It is natural and right if the desired goal is efficiency. I am only saying that the university professor tends to categorize everything in these terms, including the other professors. ("Well, of course, that's going to be her argument, she's a postmodern feminist.") So a philosophy professor might be a Kant guy or an epistemology specialist or – God forbid because everyone hates this type – a Wittgenstein guy. And you have certain prejudices and expectations of what that particular type is going to bring in terms of intellectual opinions and objections. And they might be wrong. We are all individuals. But we generalize and categorize, and professors do it more often and more efficiently than nearly everyone.

POLITICAL POWER AND CULTURE

When the Socialist painter Diego Rivera refused to take down a politically motivated mural (which included a portrait of Lenin) at Rockefeller Center, the Rockefellers had the mural destroyed and paid him off in full. They then funded abstract art, possibly for aesthetic reasons, but also because *abstract art can only reference itself and cannot carry political messages.* The Rockefellers built one of the most famous museums in America, MoMA in New York City. It isn't just art, either – music also shows a steady progression into abstraction and self- reference, and arguably film does as well. Lest one believe that I am exaggerating or misrepresented the interest of wealthy elites, it has been confirmed for some twenty years that the CIA *invested* in modern art.

For decades in art circles it was either a rumor or a joke, but now it is confirmed as a fact. The Central Intelligence Agency used American modern art --- including the works of such artists as Jackson Pollock, Robert Motherwell, Willem de Kooning and Mark Rothko – as a weapon in the Cold War. In the manner of a Renaissance prince – except that it acted secretly – the CIA fostered and promoted American Abstract Expressionist painting around the world for more than 20 years.

...decision to include culture and art in the US Cold War arsenal was taken as soon as the CIA was founded in 1947. Dismayed at the appeal communism still had for many intellectuals and artists in the West, the new agency set up a division, the Propaganda Assets Inventory, which at its peak could influence more than 800 newspapers, magazines and public information organisations. They joked that it was like a Wurlitzer jukebox: when the CIA pushed a button it could hear whatever tune it wanted playing across the world.[xxi]

The main failure of paradigms in political analysis is the failure to have an accurate model for how power operates within the system. Everyone, including academics, underestimates it. There seems to be an underlying assumption that humans will not believe as selfish 'rational' agents when given great responsibility. Just the way every police officer that kills a person of color or rapes a homeless person is deemed a 'bad apple,' the occasional scandalous senator is treated as an aberration. Which gives wonderful cover for the state when it wishes to fund a certain type of cultural propaganda in museums. Or kill presidents.

Michael Parenti expresses very well the issue:

> ...if the U.S. public manifests no mobilized opposition to the existing social order or some major aspect of it, this is treated as evidence of a freely developed national consensus. What is ruled out *a priori* is the possibility of a manipulated consensus, a controlled communication universe in which certain opinions are given generous plays and others...are systematically ignored, suppressed, or misrepresented.[xxii]

The overriding point is, of course, that conspiracy theorists begin essentially believing in the same basic tenets of civil society. It's when the individual spots an odd shoe beneath the curtain, or an odd wisp of smoke on the side, that causes him or her to yank it down to see old man Oz. That breaks the paradigm.

Conspiracy research is what allows people to see and understand the state.

In my experience, conspiracy theorists are not delusional or duped. They tend to be more like Roddy Piper in *They Live* after he puts on the alien sunglasses and concludes: "It figures it would be something like this." They've had their eyes opened and the only question is, how many cracks are there? What else is the government hiding?

The answer is plenty. Very often, a person's first reaction to hearing that you think Oswald didn't kill John F. Kennedy, or that 9/11 was some other conspiracy theory rather than Bin Laden's Spelunkers Learned to Fly, they will say something like "the government is so incompetent, they can't keep a secret for two minutes. Hell, look at Monica Lewinsky and the cigar. Look at Watergate and Nixon. The reason we've heard about these things is because you can't keep a conspiracy going."

Of course this ignores the fact that we all know that covert operations have been a part of U.S. foreign policy at least since World War II. (Indeed, they go back a lot further than that, but for now let's just say WWII.) The next question to ask is: *are there any covert operations in the last 75 years of which the American people are unaware?* In other words, do we know *everything* the CIA and various agencies have covertly undertaken in all that time? If the NSA and CIA the FBI and Defense Intelligence and the Office of Naval Intelligence all suddenly declassified their files, do you think that all of those files would contain *no new information?* Would we learn nothing?

If you think the answer is yes, then you can get off the train here. Take the Yellow Brick Road to your right.

If you think the answer is no, we have some places to go together.

CARDINAL WOOLSEY: "You're a constant regret to me, Thomas. If you could just see facts flat-on, without that horrible moral squint... With a little common sense you could have made a statesman. "

-John Bolt, *A Man for All Seasons*

FACTS AND FICTION IN *ALL THE PRESIDENT'S MEN*

The year 1976 saw the release of two films whose scripts are among the greatest ever written – *Taxi Driver*, by Paul Schrader, and *Network*, by Paddy Chayefsky – as well as William Goldman's screenplay for *All the President's Men*, the subject of this current essay. Goldman ended up taking the Oscar, although there is more to the story, as we shall see.

The essential paradox of *All the President's Men* is that it is a brilliant, superbly crafted film which happens to be dedicated to telling a fairy tale version of the Watergate incident. The writing, performances, camerawork, and direction are all pitched at a level that suggests absolute fidelity, with convincing layers of incidental detail, and yet it all falls apart under analysis. I think the reasons for that are interesting, but before we begin, I want to lay out some of the pitfalls that are inherent in analyzing any film that purports to describe an historical situation.

The first thing to understand is that a movie is a movie. No matter how well done, a movie – if it is to work at all – must be dedicated to its own narrative above all other things. In constructing a screenplay, incidental detail that does not propel the narrative gets chucked. If you're ever watching a picture based on something you know well, and you are wondering why they left something out, that is the most likely reason. Historical films often telescope events and combine several characters into one and so on. They must in order to tell a story, which is not the same thing as history. When history and story clash, it is history that loses. It's only when the changes are gratuitous or preposterous that criticism becomes justified. For example, one of the ironies of Oliver Stone's *JFK* is that it was attacked as untruthful, but it's one of the best Hollywood historical dramas ever made. Very few pictures that were "based on true events" could survive the production of an annotated screenplay with footnotes, as *JFK* did, whether you're talking about *El Cid* or *Titanic* or Jerry Bruckheimer's grotesquely inane *Pearl Harbor*.

However, having said that, when evaluating whether a film did well in covering historical events, you can't demand faithfulness to the details but you should demand faithfulness to the reality. That may sound like a contradiction, but it isn't. When Steve Wozniak was asked about Aaron Sorkin's script for the film *Steve Jobs*, he said "None of this happened, but it's all true." *That* is the point. Did the film get the essence of the story right? A film can screw up the facts and still tell the truth – in fact, that's what the best historical films do. If you want better than that, then you're gonna need a different medium. Read a book.

There's another aspect to this evaluation I want to get into for a moment before we proceed. One of the basic questions of any film is "How much of what I'm seeing is intentional?" Film is inherently a collaborative medium and it is not, despite what the *auteur* theory says, solely the vision of a single director. (Like any rule, there are a handful of exceptions, like David Lynch.) It's true that the director makes all the key decisions, generally speaking, but there are a huge number of people working to give the director as many as options as possible to match that vision. And there are accidents both happy and unhappy. Film critics generally treat everything on the screen as intentional, which is a good way to proceed, but reality doesn't always work like that. Here's what I mean: After the well-known conspiracy author Uri Dowbenko died, I picked up his collection *Hoodwinked: Watching Movies with Eyes Wide Open* and found it a little disappointing. Dowbenko makes some interesting points here and there, but overall he posits a level of control over the material that simply doesn't exist for 99% of films. He didn't know enough about the business to realize that many decisions are based on things that have nothing to do with the story concept or to seed certain ideas to the public. Sometimes it's because the actor brought in their pet screenwriter to give them a scene that makes he or she look better, or because the producer wanted a box of tobacco in the shot to make a little money. Paraphrasing Freud, sometimes a cigar is just product placement.

On the other hand, are there mystic and/or secret messages going on in some films? Undoubtedly. The picture I worked on went to the Jung center for an analysis of black/white and up/down symbolism in the screenplay. The resulting analysis was quite fascinating and shows that there are artistic people who do pay attention to such things. But do checkerboard floor patterns get repeatedly obsessively in Hollywood films because of their Masonic context or because designers like checkerboard patterns? Good question. Sometimes it clearly seems like design to me. However, in a film like Rian Johnson's *The Brothers Bloom,* for example, the content is so stuffed to the gills with Masonic and Enochian references that at some point one must assume they are all deliberate. And then you combine that with the fact that Johnson had never directed a hit before he was given *Star Wars* to play with, and maybe you do ask the question.

OK, end of preamble. Keeping this in mind, let's look at *All the President's Men*.

The project took seed during an incident that occurred when Robert Redford was working on the satirical Michael Ritchie film *The Candidate*. As part of the film, there were real press people following him around as he pretended to be a candidate. One night, over drinks, Redford talked with the reporters about why they were following him around instead of sniffing around Watergate like these two reporters from the Post, Bob Woodward and Carl Bernstein. After getting back some cynical replies, Redford lost his temper: "So you guys are gonna sit here on your ass, you're not gonna do anything about it but smoke your cigars and have our free booze and write a superficial story about what I'm doing and that's it?"[1]

Redford goes home and tells his buddy William Goldman about the exchange and about doing a film on Watergate. Goldman gets excited. Redford then sets up a meeting with Woodward and Bernstein, and after

[1] Brown, Jared, *Alan J. Pakula: His Films and His Life* (BackStage Books: NY 2005), 149.

feeling each other out they decide the project could be a go. It was decided Goldman would write it. He'd already worked with Redford twice, on *The Great Waldo Pepper* and the picture that turned Redford into a star, *Butch Cassidy and the Sundance Kid*. He was seemingly perfect. Dustin Hoffman signed on for Bernstein. Then they landed on a director, Alan J. Pakula (after turning down William Friedkin, of *The French Connection* and *Exorcist* fame, who wanted to do it) who was perfect, a master of tone in films like *Klute* and *The Parallax View*. And they had one of the all-time great cinematographers Gordon Willis to shoot the film, who had worked with Pakula before and shot *The Godfather* films for Francis Ford Coppola. The contribution of Willis is hard to overstate, as the dry and realistic look of the film, with its bold shadows, has an enormous effect on the film's atmosphere.

Goldman's screenplay became the source of a lot of contention. A brilliant writer (he would go on to write more classics such as *Marathon Man* and *The Princess Bride*, among other things), he had become known for writing a Western buddy comedy and the fear was that he was writing *Carl Bernstein and the Sundance Woodward*. But he had solved the screenplay's structure (discarding the last half of the book, ending on a screwup by the two reporters) and also found his way to two key elements to help the audience. One was the famous phrase, "follow the money." The other was the person who said it, Deep Throat, eventually played by Hal Holbrook in the picture. The Deep Throat scenes in the underground garage are the silliest scenes in the film, although they still play because of the high levels of the performers and the direction. And they seemed to have occurred because Bob Woodward had an outsize impact on the production. Which we know because Goldman said so: "I cannot overemphasize [Woodward's] contribution to the screenplay."[2] Goldman relied on him to walk him through the maze of names and connections, and of course to help dramatize Deep Throat.

Goldman was a great writer but he was not a conspiracy researcher. He was also patriotic, in a way that's not really possible anymore after the Kennedy assassination and after Watergate and after every appalling thing we've learned since. But he grew up in the 1950s and *Gunga Din* was his favorite picture and he basically wanted to write about heroes in a sincere way. Years later he would be approached to write the screenplay for the adaptation of Tom Wolfe's *The Right Stuff*, but he ended up turning it down because the director, Phil Kaufman, had a cynical take on the material.[3] Whereas he wanted to write about how exciting the whole damn thing was.

[2] Goldman, William, *Adventures in the Screen Trade* (Warner Books: NY 1984), 218.

Anyway, he's having trouble with the script and things are coming to loggerheads. So one day Goldman shows up to a production meeting and in the room are Carl Bernstein and his girlfriend, Nora Ephron. The *writer* Nora Ephron, who would go on to write *When Harry Met Sally* and *Sleepless in Seattle* and *You've Got Mail* (and incidentally a terrific Mike Nichols film, *Silkwood*, which also has conspiratorial overtones and is based on real life). Ephron and Bernstein are beaming because she's got a snazzy new script she wrote for the picture. Which everybody thinks can be married to the Goldman version. Except Goldman, who exits stage left. (One leftover beat from the Ephron script can be seen in the movie, in that Bernstein is extremely attractive to women.)

After that, Woodward and Pakula ended up doing their own script together, which was then stitched together with everything else and *that* became the film *All the President's Men*.

Which worked like gangbusters.

It happens. Moviemaking seems to be one of those things where there are at least five clear rules, but no one knows what they are. *Jaws* was famously a disastrous production until people saw the thing. Hence Goldman's most famous remark: "Nobody knows

---

[3] Ibid, 241.

anything." It could have been different. There were competing scenes shot for both Redford and Hoffman that showed their personal relationships. Movie star ego stuff. If those scenes had been left in the picture, terrible. Fortunately, saner heads prevailed.

THE DIFFERENCES

There are many fascinating differences between the script of *All the President's Men* and the film, (for one thing, Post publisher Katharine Graham makes an appearance in the script) but I want to focus on just two. One because it reinforces one thing we have learned about the production process, which is that Bob Woodward had a large footprint. He had a large footprint on it when Goldman was working on the script, and then an even bigger one once Goldman was out. Which makes sense, since *All the President's Men* is essentially the CIA-ONI version of what happened during Watergate.

Both differences I want to focus on involve the character of Donald Segretti, the "ratfucker" who handles the details of operations against Edmund Muskie, among others. In the film, Segretti is a key figure because once the reporters locate him, that leads to the "dirty tricks" and helps to make sense of how Watergate fits into the pattern. Of course, the pattern they discover is the wrong pattern, in the sense that it leads to the idea that these dirty tricks are deployed in response to the upcoming election, rather than business as usual in a world in which high crimes are being committed all the time. Which is the most basic lie of *All the President's Men*, which is that the bad guys (Nixon and his cronies) were undone by the good guys (Woodstein), when in fact almost everybody involved is a bad guy of one shade or another.

Anyway, the first scene I want to focus on is right after the meeting with Segretti. In Goldman's script, Bernstein meets him alone and a lot of the dialogue is exactly the same. It ends with Segretti making that rueful remark about just getting out of the Army and getting a call to serve the President. However, in the script, the scene cuts to this scene:

```
WOODWARD AND BERNSTEIN

Back in D.C., walking through the airport.

          BERNSTEIN

    What would you have done?



          WOODWARD
```

```
     You asking would I have been one of the
     President's men? (beat) I would have
     been.

As they continue on -

                    CUT TO:
```

Now that's fascinating. A little on the nose? Sure. But it also reflects a key insight into Bob Woodward's personality. He wishes to be recruited. He wishes to serve. He does serve. Throughout his career, Woodward has served the CIA many times. And maybe you cut the scene because you don't like the scene, and maybe Woodward rejects the scene because it's a little too close to the truth. Anyway, it didn't make the movie, and I think we can see why.

My friend Joseph McBride once told me that, when this film was being made, he was sent down to do an interview with Alan Pakula for a magazine piece. McBride knocked on Pakula's door, who refused to do the interview owing to time restraints. However, Joe did get in one question, which was that had Pakula, by any chance, heard the rumors that Woodward was connected to intelligence? Pakula responded that he had, but if he started thinking that way he'd go crazy.

The second change from script to screen also involves Segretti, and it's because I think the Segretti scene leads to a key insight that movie achieves in spite of itself. The main difference between the way Goldman writes the scene and the way Pakula shoots it is that Pakula divides the scene in two. Goldman has the two guys in one scene talking through the implications of Segretti, whereas Pakula has them first in a taxi and then going through receipts together in the room and it's very effective.

However, in their dialogue, there is one excision that is made in the context of the discussion. Because when Bernstein is telling Woodward about how he got the tip that leads to Segretti, he says the following:

```
BERNSTEIN

...for the first time I'm beginning
to feel like a fucking reporter -
Woodward, I got a tip. A guy
called me up with a tip
[carefully] - someone named Donald
Segretti contacted a bunch of
lawyers and asked them if they'd
like to go to work with him
screwing up the Democrats, dirty
tricks, shit like that. The FBI
knows about Segretti - Howard Hunt
made a bunch of phone calls to him
- they interrogated him, but on
```

> account of Segretti wasn't
> involved in the break-in, they
> didn't follow through. But
> Segretti did a lot of traveling –
> he called these lawyers from
> different places, and he told them
> the Republicans knew what he was
> doing.

Although Pakula handles the scene extremely well, there is one omission that mars it in comparison to the Goldman version. Pakula's version omits the mention of Howard Hunt.

It's a curious thing about *All the President's Men* in that the way Woodward first gets caught up in the story is through the arrest of the Watergate burglars, including E. Howard Hunt, and their pursuit of Hunt's library research into Edward Kennedy and the Chappaquiddick incident. (See the past two issues of garrison for more on that.) Now E. Howard Hunt leads back to the Bay of Pigs and – of course – the JFK assassination, if you play your cards right. But Bob Woodward was determined *not* to play those particular cards right and neither is the movie.

Interesting.

However, I want to give the film credit where it's due, even if it does so by accident. That's because it's also in this scene that we learn an excellent method of doing research that is applicable to a great many other things. Woodward and Bernstein begin going through Segretti's travel records, and they find that he has been at the same place at the same time that numerous embarrassing incidents have taken place against Democrats, and those records begin a year before Watergate ever happened. Which allows them to recontextualize what happens at Watergate into a larger picture.

There's just one problem. They don't recontextualize the situation enough. They don't pull back far enough on the method. Because you don't just check Segretti's receipts. You check Hunt's. Hunt leads to Massachusetts and a lot of other places.

And then you start going further. Take, for example, Arthur Bremer, who shot George Wallace, at a time when Wallace represented a reasonable threat to Nixon's presidency.

Bremer had never had money and hadn't been known to take trips. In January of 1972, Bremer suddenly quit his job, right after purchasing a Charter Arms .38 revolver. The day after he quit, on February 1, Bremer purchased another new pistol, a Browning 9mm. He didn't use that gun, however, but the Charter Arms to shoot at Wallace, having concealed the Browning in his Rambler automobile. (Yes, a Rambler.) Bremer then started making trips, including staying two nights at the Waldorf-Astoria in April. He drove to Milwaukee at one point, staying long enough to purchase membership in the ACLU. In May he withdrew two books on the RFK assassination from the library and a couple of weeks later allegedly shot at George Wallace and was arrested. Here is one notable paragraph from the New York Times article:

"His father has told the Federal Bureau of Investigation, a source said, that his thrifty son, who had a savings account at the Mitchell Street State Bank in Milwaukee, had withdrawn substantial sums in recent months and had been living off the money. Bank officials declined to discuss the account."[4]

Imagine you are Woodward and Bernstein in the scene where they are reviewing Segretti's receipts. Imagine that they are reviewing this information about Bremer instead. What conclusions would they draw? What conclusions *should* they draw?

Check John Hinckley's receipts. Check Mark David Chapman's receipts. (You'll find Chapman and Hinckley are connected through an interesting outfit called World Vision, among other things.) In my previous article on the Chappaquiddick incident, I pointed out that Ted Kennedy had been the victim of an assassination attempt by one Suzanne Osgood in 1979. It was a fairly

[4] "Now, Arthur Bremer is Known." *The New York Times*, May 22, 1972.

minor incident, but I followed up the receipts on her too, and guess what? Money and travel. How about that.

All the President's Men – despite its many deceptions and Hollywood issues – shows one excellent method for research. And it works. And that, in my opinion, makes the film worthwhile beyond the obvious excellence of its execution.

Follow the money, sure. But also, check the receipts.

"Private enterprise cannot be maintained in the age of democracy; it is conceivable only if the people have a sound idea of authority and personality...All the worldly goods we possess we owe to that struggle of the chosen...We must not forget that all the benefits of culture must be introduced more or less with an iron fist."

-Adolf Hitler, 1933

"McDonald's cannot flourish without McDonnell Douglas, the designer of the F-15."

-Thomas Friedman, economist

HOLLYWOOD AND NICHOLAS SCHOU'S *SPOOKED*

1.

Sometime during production of the film *All the President's Men,* the director Alan J. Pakula fired the screenwriter, William Goldman. This isn't especially notable – writers are always the first people to get fired off any production – although this wasn't just any screenwriter. In his book *Adventures in the Screen Trade,* Goldman writes that it seemed like everybody on the planet knew he'd been having issues with it. He says he happened to meet Walter Cronkite during this period, and the only thing Cronkite said to him was "I hear you're having script trouble."

In 1976, Goldman won the Oscar for writing *All the President's Men,* despite having been fired off the picture.

Other writers had done passes on the script, most notably Nora Ephron. Ephron was dating Carl Bernstein at the time, the reporter portrayed by Dustin Hoffman in the picture, who in turn was the partner to Bob

Woodward, played by Robert Redford. Goldman later observed that Bernstein sure seemed to be "catnip to the ladies" in Ephron's scenes.

Did Goldman deserve the Oscar? He definitely built the structure to carry the story, which is not easy to do. *All the President's Men* is – aesthetically – a terrific movie, and it starts with the writing. Jason Robards got an Oscar for stealing every scene he's in, but honestly the part is gift-wrapped for him. There is snappy dialogue, some terrific reversals, and a gripping story. It's become a model for this sort of film – the recent Oscar-winning *Spotlight* showed its influence, for example.

There's only one problem. **All the President's Men is a lie**. It's the setting in stone of the public face of the Richard Nixon scandal, told with the help of Woodward and his ex-ONI buddies and Al Haig. It glorifies the myth of "Woodstein," intrepid reporters taking down a criminal president. It also did for Bob Woodward what the JFK assassination did for Dan Rather – provide a platform to kick off a career serving the state through the media.

Hollywood has had a complicated relationship with the government for a long time, partly for reasons of actual patriotism and partly because of money. (It's always at least partly the money.) Right now on Netflix there is a wonderful documentary series *Five Came Back*, about how great directors like John Ford, Frank Capra, and John Huston, among others, helped make films supporting the U.S. against the Nazis. They took their job seriously in this regard. Joseph McBride details the background, for example, of the making of the film *Mr. Smith Goes to Washington* in his wonderful book *Frank Capra: The Catastrophe of Success*. Capra, a complex figure if there ever was one, felt conflicted by the thought he might have made a picture casting his adopted country in a negative light. "When a prominent man like the ambassador of England says this is going to hurt the war effort, that was serious. Would it do that? I wanted to do what was right." (McBride, 423).

However, it's one thing to make pro-American films when the cause is just. When Indiana Jones says, "Nazis. I hate these guys," we agree.

Unfortunately, there are some Hollywood directors who are eager to cooperate with the U.S. in favor of more dubious causes, as with Kathryn Bigelow in *The Hurt Locker* and *Zero Dark Thirty*, or Michael Bay making the military look terribly exciting for young men in the *Transformers* series. Clint Eastwood took up the ridiculous cause of invading Grenada in *Heartbreak Ridge* and the Pentagon backed *Top Gun*, essentially a long commercial for fighter pilots. Ben Affleck celebrated the CIA in *Argo* and was rewarded for it by both the public and the Academy. Tom Hanks infamously backed Vincent Bugliosi – a project that united the typically fractious JFK research community.

On the other side, films opposing the American military-intelligence-complex tend to face stiff opposition and little funding. Oliver Stone has been the exception rather than the rule in this arena, as the best political films tend to be either foreign or small-budget enterprises, such Costa-Gavras's *Z*. While controversy can help sell a picture, criticizing established structures of power isn't the kind of controversy producers like. This even extends to actors. When Jean Seberg, the gorgeous ingénue from Jean-Luc Godard's famous film *Breathless*, got pregnant by a Black Panther, the FBI tried to drive her to suicide.[xxiii]

2.

In the last few years, a slate of books about the unhealthy relationship between domestic intelligence agencies and media centers have emerged. Nicholas Schou's *Spooked* is one of the newest, and it comes with heavy praise: a foreword by David Talbot, as well as endorsements from the likes of Oliver Stone and Peter

Dale Scott. Schou's own *bona fides* are formidable, having worked as an investigative journalist and written the Gary Webb biography *Kill the Messenger*, which was made into the film starring Jeremy Renner.

The subtitle of the book is *How the CIA Manipulates the Media and Hoodwinks Hollywood*. Unfortunately, this subtitle is itself something of a hoodwink. A short book (less than 150 pages), the content really consists of a survey of some of the major news stories of the last half-century or so. The chapters deal with various aspects, for example, of WikiLeaks and its relation to the media, Julian Assange, Edward Snowden, the Iraqi war scandals, the Church committee, Seymour Hersh on the Osama bin Laden raid, Robert Parry and his work, and a short summation of the Gary Webb crack-cocaine CIA scandal. These are all worthy topics, and deserve longer treatments than they get here (and in fact did, since as noted Schou also wrote the Webb biography.)

The short length of the book means that each topic is dealt with in a superficial manner. For example, he mentions that when CIA agent Valerie Plame was "outed," it was by Richard Armitage (Schou 67). However, he gives no further information on Armitage, who was Assistant Secretary of Defense for International Security Affairs under Ronald Reagan and a key player in the Iran-Contra scandal. In addition to that, he also met with General Mahmoud Ahmed, the leader of the Pakistani ISI, the week of 9/11. General Ahmed is important because he ordered a wire transfer of $100,000 to the alleged leader of the Saudi-Arabian hijackers, Mohammed Atta. There is a wealth of information lurking behind the stories that appear in *Spooked*, and while it's understandable that he can't get to everything, Schou misses some key aspects of the particular events he is trying to summarize. He also fails to cite much information in the way of demonstrating that CIA "manipulates the media" or "hoodwinks Hollywood."

First of all, this is a dubious premise to being with; for the most part, the CIA more or less *is* the media quite often. We know because of Carl Bernstein's famous article in *Rolling Stone* that the CIA quite often pays journalists directly to work for the agency. And Schou does mention this in his book, as well as citing examples like William Paley at CBS and other stories that are already pretty well known.

Also, Hollywood isn't hoodwinked; like any other business, there are people who are willing to play ball and others who aren't. For example, when it was announced that Antwone Fuqua was going to make a picture about heroin being smuggled into the United States in the caskets of American soldiers during the

Vietnam War, I got excited. Fuqua tried to push the boundaries while he was hot off *Training Day*. Not hot enough, alas; Universal fired him, replacing him with Ridley Scott. Scott made *American Gangster* into a fairly standard cop and criminal picture, soft-pedaling the elements that might make the state nervous.

This kind of thing happens all the time.

So let's get back to Schou. He should have a deep insight into at least one project in particular, right? *Kill the Messenger*. I remember when the film was announced, because Peter Landesman, who had written and directed the disastrous JFK assassination film *Parkland*, was also announced as the director. This had the smell of cover-up all over it. Landesman, who had never helmed anything remotely the size of *Parkland* before, made a bad film that tanked at the box office.

When *Parkland* was still in pre-production, I had been hired to work as a research and script consultant to a film called *Dallas in Wonderland*, directed by Ryan Page. Over the course of three years or more, we did location scouting, casting, and – while we were waiting to get *Dallas* off the ground – ended up making a documentary with Oliver Stone called *King Kill 63*. Anyway, I was in L.A. a lot during that time, and in a lot of meetings, and that *Parkland* script was everywhere.

Everybody had seen it. And everybody said, "hey, listen, don't tell anybody, but I saw this script..." It was well-known in the industry that the script was a pile of crap.

At the time, the idea was that *Dallas in Wonderland* would be the anti-*Parkland*. And the script was good. It would have been a thriller in the tradition of 70's thrillers like *The Parallax View* and, especially, Brian de Palma's *Blow Out* (itself a quasi-remake of Antonioni's *Blowup*, a film that alluded to the JFK assassination directly). Anyway, during this period I learned a lot about how films are made – in terms of the production aspect – and all the things that go into how decisions get made in Hollywood.

Mostly, it's accountants. You'd think that with a modestly budgeted picture (say $12-15 million) you could more or less cast who you want. You can't. There were actors that I thought would be great to play the lead, for example, but we couldn't do it because they had no juice in China. Or they're considered TV actors (see the James Toback documentary *Seduced and Abandoned* for more on this). If we were going to get the picture made, we needed a male lead and that male lead needed to be a big star.

But that's another story. **The point is, *Parkland* had nothing going for it.** The director, Peter Landesman, was not a name director. The script was bad – even

Hollywood people who liked the script thought it was bad. There's no foreign. (JFK assassination pictures don't travel.) There were no big stars to open (some fine actors, but nobody like Leo.)

The thing got made anyway.

That's what I'd loved to hear about from Schou. Why? *Parkland* disobeyed the natural laws of how Hollywood pictures get made. How did that happen?

This is what Schou says about Landesman:

> Landesman, who worked as a foreign correspondent in Pakistan after 9/11 and wrote national security stories for the New York Times magazine, was equipped with a better bullshit detector than most filmmakers by the time he got to Hollywood. 'I have had a number of dealings with the CIA, both as a journalist and a screenwriter, he said. 'I quickly learned that I could never, ever, take what any [CIA] officer says at face value. They are hardwired to deflect, even off the record.'[xxiv]

I felt like Jim Garrison (Kevin Costner) in *JFK* reading

this part. **Ask the question! Ask the question!**

What's the question Schou needed to ask Landesman?

If you learned you can't trust anything the CIA tells you, why the hell did you make *Parkland*?

The question doesn't get asked.

The punchline is that this director who laid an egg with *Parkland* makes *Kill the Messenger,* and it ends up being a solid film.[xxv]

Because Hollywood is weird. And complicated. And who knows what back-room deals got engineered – maybe it was "do this one for us, and we'll let you do one for you." There's a story there somewhere. In the end, both films got buried.

For Schou to write this book, on this topic, without even getting to the details of how his own book got made into a movie is inexplicable and inexcusable.

The movie I worked on, *Dallas in Wonderland,* might never get made. The documentary I co-wrote and co-produced, *King Kill 63,* closed the Dallas International Film Festival at the Texas Theatre and played great. I answered audience questions afterward until they literally kicked us out of the theatre. The reason nobody can see it is long and complicated and I'll write that book someday. Meanwhile, I cross my fingers that it gets released.

One last anecdote.

When Ryan and I arrived in Dallas for the DIFF showing in 2015, we had an email waiting for us from the Sixth Floor Museum. They were very disturbed about our showing. We were using footage that *belonged* to them — by which they meant, essentially, all extant footage even vaguely involving the Kennedy assassination. They suggested we not show the film that night unless we were prepared to pay them for, for example, using the Zapruder film. These were not nominal fees, and this already was an expensive film — we had shot with a full film crew all over the country.

We discussed our options, legal and otherwise. I talked to another documentary filmmaker friend who had recently gone through this with the Sixth Floor. At the end of the day, we decided to show it.

The morning after our showing at the Texas Theatre, we got another email. The representative they sent from the Sixth Floor had liked the film, they said, and hoped we could work something out in the future. The person they'd sent had stayed for the Q&A afterward but declined to identify himself.

A little creepy, that.

One more aside: when we were location scouting for *Dallas in Wonderland*, it was decided that I would not go with the producers that day because they were concerned Gary Mack or somebody on the Sixth Floor staff would recognize me. (I don't think that would have happened, but they didn't want to take chances.) So I went out with the 2nd unit crew to shoot some stuff in Lee Harvey Oswald's jail cell. Anyway, when we all met again that night, the producers said the Sixth Floor had a large board set up in the Sixth Floor offices that showed *every single film or television project on the topic of JFK* that was ongoing. Even if it was just in the option stage.

We were on that list, and we hadn't even been announced in *Variety* yet at that point.

There's a lot more to this story, much of which I can't tell for various reasons, but the main point is that my expectation would be that Mr. Schou would have some insight into *Kill the Messenger*.

He doesn't. He says he wasn't at all involved. Okay.

3.

Having said all that, this is not a bad book. It just doesn't really live up to the title and subtitle. However, if you're looking for a short overview of important aspects of journalism and the government, there is good information here. It would make a good gift for someone who is getting introduced to this material and, as a quick read, does efficiently get across some of the key aspects of the Gary Webb story, for example.

Schou also directs attention to one of the real classics in this genre, Frances Stonor Saunders's *The CIA and the Cultural Cold War*. That's a great book every researcher should have. There are many other fine ones, like Hugh Wilford's *The Mighty Wurlitzer*. Another classic, which is similar to this book but superior, is the anthology *Into the Buzzsaw* edited by Kristina Borjesson. (That book, among other things, tells the story of how William Casey bought ABC. For a while.) The books that deal best with the media in relation to the JFK assassination were written by Jim DiEugenio: *The Assassinations, Reclaiming Parkland*, and *Destiny Betrayed*. Very few other writers ever talk about people like James Phelan, for example, where you really get to see how the sausage gets made in the media.

And that might be a good place to point out what I think the key issue is with this book versus more useful books. There are different kinds of liberals. There are some liberals who are so because they believe that people shouldn't be denied basic human rights for their sexuality or religious preference, or that social security is a good thing and that having a post office and health care is desirable for everyone, rather than just those who can afford them. This is all well and good.

They stop, however, at the Kennedy assassination or anything tainted by "conspiracy." Noam Chomsky structuralist liberals can be like this, and corporate democrats run away from the word.

The trouble is, if you don't understand that the state killed JFK, and MLK, and RFK, and Malcolm X, and a whole lot of others besides, you're never really going to fundamentally understand how the world works. *Spooked* is written for the first type of liberal, and that's OK. But for people who are serious political researchers, it's not good enough. *Spooked* is limited in scope, and therefore limited in impact.

EPILOGUE

When this piece appeared in Jim DiEugenio's *Kennedys and King*, Nicholas Schou got in contact with me. He couldn't go much into details, but essentially said that the title of the book and the idea for it both came from the publisher. Which, coming from my own experience, I understand. Because what are you gonna do?

"People grow up and live in different social contexts where particular beliefs are assumed to be valid and so are rarely questioned. They do not choose from among the many possible answers to ultimate questions but simply assume that the worldview in which they have been raised is the proper one."

-Vine DeLoria, *Evolution, Creation, and Other Modern Myths*

"Henry Kissinger's deputy, William H. Sullivan, (who later was serving as the US ambassador to Iran when the hostage crisis erupted in 1979) was asked at that event why the US was still in Vietnam. He answered that it was because the US needed to control the oil in the south China Sea...what I reported was picked up by the Associated Press and went around the world on its wire... Sullivan claimed he had not made them. I produced my notes to prove that he had. Then it was claimed that Sullivan's speech to the university organization had been off the record. I produced the letter from that organization, inviting our newspaper to cover his appearance on campus."

-Joseph McBride, *Political Truth*

WHO KILLED MALCOLM X?
(OR THE SUBTLETIES OF PROPAGANDA)

On February 9, 1965, less than two weeks before he was murdered, Malcolm X was prevented from entering France. Police met him at the airport and denied him entrance into the country, forcing him to fly back to England where he had been speaking.

This was not because the French government was afraid of Malcolm X.

It was because Charles De Gaulle, the French President, was worried that the CIA would kill Malcolm while he was in the country and France would get the blame. As reported by Jim Douglass in his excellent essay, "The Murder and Martydom of Malcolm X," the reasoning was revealed by a North African diplomat to journalist Eric Norden a couple of months later. "Your CIA is beginning to murder its own citizens now," the diplomat said.[xxvi]

That story, and a great many other things, have been left out of streaming giant Netflix's new six-part documentary *Who Killed Malcolm X?* In theory, this should be the kind of thing we should cheer about: For an estimated cost of $1.2 million, featuring a terrific theme song and fine craftsmanship behind the camera, the documentary has made such a splash that there is talk it may actually reopen the case. Great, right? Let's light up cigars. Especially since, unlike the "other" major assassinations of the 1960s - JFK, MLK, and RFK - there is a substantial lack of mainstream interest. Most people, if they know anything at all about the man, assume that it was a violent man reaching a violent end, no more worthy of interest than intra-gang or mob warfare. (I have found this to be true even among political researchers, who also often demonstrate no interest in the COINTELPRO war against the Black Panthers.) If *Who Killed Malcolm X?* can get a more mainstream audience to pay attention to Malcolm's story, this is terrific news.

Unfortunately, this series falls short.

So the first thing that seemed strange is that it lacks any major scholars who have dealt with Malcolm X in a comprehensive way. If somebody gave me money to make a documentary on Malcolm X, the first thing I'd want to do is make sure we get Karl Evanzz. And Baba Zak Kondo. And Dr. Jared Ball. And the aforementioned Jim Douglass. For starters. Now the filmmakers do get a number of folks - eyewitnesses and people on the ground - who are fascinating in the stories they have to tell, but the documentary doesn't have any input from anyone who could put these stories into a bigger picture. Which is because, for whatever reason, the directors Phil Bertelsen and Rachel Dretzin choose to frame everything around the investigation of one man: Abdur-Rahman Muhammad.

Abdur-Rahman Muhammad tells us right out that he is just a regular guy, an average person who took an interest in the case and studied it for thirty years. The case never sat right with him and he was determined to get at the truth. So this series makes out Muhammad to be their Jim Garrison. Which is a fair enough approach, all things considered. And one thing he is good at is getting people to go on-camera. His status as someone from the neighborhood, as well as his Muslim faith, gives him an edge to anyone else trying to do the man-on-the-street investigation he tries to do. However, what Muhammad does throughout the series, over and over through six parts, is continually tease the uncovering of the TRUTH, just around the next corner. This leads one to believe that the sixth part in this series will be a humdinger, the thing that will develop all the various themes into a strong finish. It doesn't, but it will take a little explanation to understand why.

For the first episode I was willing to go along with the ride. It seemed like it was at least citing some of the major aspects of the case. However, somewhere through the course of the second episode or it began to dawn on me that this was going nowhere. Part of this is a question of emphasis, but unfortunately there is a large element of omission.

MALCOLM X IN HISTORY

The story of Malcolm X and his assassination requires some knowledge of his background and the background of black civil rights. To begin at the beginning, Malcolm Little was born in Omaha, Nebraska, in 1925. His father was murdered by white supremacists – the Ku Klux Klan. His father, a preacher, had been a supporter of Marcus Garvey. This is an important point, because the Garveyites were separationists. Garvey created the 'Black Star Line,' which was supposed to transport black people back to Africa. Garvey had given up on assimilation; in his eyes, only a return to the Homeland could make African Americans come back into their own dignity, as equals with one another. For a variety of reasons, the Black Star Line never worked - one of the principal ones being that the ships were often barely usable, and Garvey eventually lost his grip on reality.[xxvii] It is ultimately a tragic story.

It's also an incredibly important story, not the least of which because it underlines the two main approaches that would be taken over the course of the century - one line essentially assimilationist, and another separationist. On the assimilationist side was Garvey's rival W. E. B. DuBois, the first black man to graduate from Harvard with a doctorate. DuBois proffered a theory of the "talented tenth," the idea that black political equality and civil rights would be gained through the achievements of the best and brightest among the people. It was the sort of theory one might expect from a man with a Harvard doctorate and one unlikely to ever win mass popular support. (DuBois was a strong proponent of the "great man" theory of history, writing short profiles of men he felt were especially important. This included Abraham Lincoln and — a bit embarrassingly — Joseph Stalin.)

On the separationist side, Garvey founded the United Negro Improvement Association (UNIA), an organization which - following the Bolshevik Revolution of 1917 - grew large enough to attract the attention of a 22-year-old J. Edgar Hoover. Under President Woodrow Wilson, at the direction of John Lord O'Brian, Hoover went to work for the Alien Enemy Bureau. As would become a repeated pattern through the years, government agents were sent to infiltrate UNIA and retrieve intelligence. By 1919, Hoover himself grew to be the head of the General Intelligence Division of the

Bureau of Investigation.[xxviii] The next year he joined the Federal Lodge No. 1 in Washington, D.C. and by 1924 he was director - at the age of 29. That is to say, Hoover's personal history mirrors the rise of black civil rights movements of the 20th century, and his first connection with it was conflated with Communism and anti-Americanism.

Returning to Malcolm, he would wind up in prison in 1946. As related in his classic autobiography, as "told to" Alex Haley, he met a man called John Bembry in prison who converted him to the Nation of Islam (NOI). He became an American Muslim. This is not the same thing as mainstream Muslim faith, but a peculiar strain of Islam with somewhat tenuous connections to other strains.

Malcolm Little became Malcolm X, disposing of his "slave name." The NOI, led by the Honorable Elijah Muhammad, dictated that adherents get rid of their surnames since they had nothing to do with their origins but rather served as a kind of American costume. It was no accident that so many American founder names grew to become stereotypically "black" names - Jefferson, Washington, Franklin, and the like. It is natural to bestow a name of distinction on oneself, lacking other options; however, in the case of black Americans, this state of affairs did not emerge from an adoption but from a kidnapping.

THE DOCUMENTARY

This is roughly the point at which the documentary begins. It details the rise of Malcolm X as a public figure from the late 1950s to his ultimate murder in 1965. Malcolm, later Malik El-Shabazz, gave everything to the Nation of Islam, and received everything in return - his home, his wife, his place in the community. However, Malcolm became so popular that he eventually posed a threat to the Elijah Muhammad and his sons, and they broke with one another. Eventually there were threats and actual violence as Malcolm revealed that Elijah Muhammad had slept with several of his young secretaries and fathered children with them. This revelation had little effect on his believers except to galvanize their opposition to Malcolm.

And it's this internal Muslim conflict that drives the film. In interview after interview shown in the documentary, Abdur-Rahman pursues the questions that personally bother him, which involve (for the most part) concerns about the importation of New Jersey mosque members to murder Malcolm. Curiously, however, he does not explore the fact that the current head of the NOI, Louis Farrakhan, has a connection. The former Louis Walcott, Farrakhan wrote and distributed a document which spelled out his feelings following Malcolm's betrayal of his former master:

The die is set, and Malcolm shall not escape, especially after such evil, foolish talk about his benefactor (Elijah Muhammad) ... Such a man as Malcolm is worthy of death and would have met with death if it had not been for Muhammad's confidence in Allah for victory over the enemies.[xxix]

There is no doubt of a climate of hate surrounding Malcolm with respect to his former associates within the Nation of Islam. However, there was also continual harassment and violence emanating from the police and FBI.

To take one example, in January of 1958 a pair of detectives working for the NYC police went to Malcolm's apartment without a warrant to search for a woman called Margaret Dorsey. Malcolm told the detectives he wanted to see a warrant. Instead, the detectives opened fire on the apartment where his pregnant wife was also living. Although they did not hit anyone, this brought home the level of danger surrounding the minister even at this relatively early date.[xxx]

However, in addition to these direct assaults, there

were plots being developed within the government. CIA Director Richard Helms had made tracking Malcolm a "priority" beginning in 1964.[xxxi] Strikingly, this was three years before the CIA began its own MH/CHAOS program, which was designed to track and destroy left wing and black resistance movements, and which began via the involvement of Helms and another name familiar to JFK researchers: James Jesus Angleton.[xxxii]

Further plots arose out of COINTELPRO[xxxiii], a program designed specifically to overthrow, neutralize, or kill black leaders and replace them with FBI-approved figures. (In other words, to mirror domestically what covert operations had been doing successfully in other countries.) William Sullivan, J. Edgar Hoover's handpicked assistant for all investigative operations. Sullivan, through COINTELPRO, successfully infiltrated and damaged left-wing movements in the period between 1956 and 1971.

In 1964, Sullivan circulated a memo proposing that a "new national Negro leader" be selected after first destroying their three main targets: Elijah Muhammad, Malcolm X, and MLK. Sullivan even had an idea for their replacement: a corporate lawyer named Samuel R. Pierce, Jr.[xxxiv]

Later that same year, a rumor circulated that "Black Muslims" were planning to assassinate Lyndon Johnson.

According to news reports, Malcolm X was wanted for questioning. Malcolm immediately realized what was going on - and although he had been meeting Alex Haley to discuss his life, he did not want to discuss the Johnson assassination rumor. If ever there was a day to be a little frightened, that would have been the day. He would have realized the scale of the forces aligned against him.

Karl Evanzz notes that Elijah Muhammad would have understood the meaning as well:

> For Muhammad, the meaning of the report was readily apparent. He knew that the allegations were a fabrication, but he also realized the underlying message: if the FBI leaked a story linking Malcolm X with Lee Harvey Oswald and the Fair Play for Committee, Muhammad would once again find himself in Washington facing the microphones of the House Un-American Activities Commission. Another HUAC probe could land both him and Malcolm X in prison...There was no way he could permit Malcolm X to return to the Nation of Islam.[xxxv]

Similarly, in July of 1964, Malcolm went to an outdoor restaurant in Cairo. His food tasted strange to him and he realized that he recognized his waiter from having seen him before in New York. He had been poisoned. He was rushed to the hospital, had his stomach pumped, and barely survived. Malcolm of course understood that the Nation of Islam did not have global agents. This had to be a U.S. government operation.[xxxvi]

THE NIGHT OF THE ASSASSINATION

For the most part, the documentary shows the basic facts of the actual murder of Malcolm X with reasonable fidelity, although once again there are serious omissions. The assassination took place on February 21, 1965, in the Audubon Ballroom in New York City. Malcolm had been invited to give a speech at this location.

The Audubon consisted of a long hall. Malcolm was on one side on a stage with a podium.
At the other end of the hall, facing him, was the main entrance to the building. In between some folding chairs had been set up.

Before the talk begins, as Malcolm arrives at the podium, there was a fake altercation between two men – draws people attention to them. One of the men yelled, "Get your hands out of my pockets!" Meanwhile, a smoke bomb was thrown into the room.

First, one man with a shotgun ran up to Malcolm and shot him. He then ran out a side door.

Then, two men with .45 caliber pistols ran out and shot Malcolm some more, while he was on the ground. They fled out the back way, out the main entrance. One of the men who ran out the back was caught by the people outside, who proceeded to beat him almost to death.

The documentary makes a big deal out of revealing the identity of William X Bradley as the man with the shotgun who murdered Malcolm X. However, this is not a reveal to anyone who followed the case. Also, the fact that he lived in the neighborhood and had been brought up on charges was well known. One of the bright spots in Manning Marable's book, for all its flaws, is that Marable points out that Bradley appears to have been protected by the government - even years later:

On April 11, 1968, the Livingston National Bank of Livingston, New Jersey, was robbed by three masked men brandishing three handguns and one sawed-off shotgun. They escaped with over $12,500. The following year Bradley and a second man, James Moore, were charged with the bank robbery and were brought to trial. Bradley, however, received privileged treatment, and he retained his own attorney separate from Moore. The charges against him were ultimately dismissed; meanwhile, after a first trial ending in a hung jury, Moore was convicted in a second trial.

Bradley's special treatment by the criminal justice system in 1969-1970 raises the question of whether he was an FBI informant, either after the assassination of Malcolm X or very possibly even before. It would perhaps explain why Bradley took a different exit from the murder scene than the two other shooters, shielding him from the crowd's retaliation. It suggests that Bradley and possibly other Newark mosque members may have actively collaborated on the shooting with local law enforcement and/or the FBI.[xxxvii]

One of the real missed opportunities of the documentary is the stunning interviews with Corey Booker and the Lieutenant Governor in episode five of the series. The filmmakers spring the news to Booker that Bradley, the alleged assassin of Malcolm X, appeared in one of his campaign videos. When asked whether he knows Bradley, Booker says yes and that he's a wonderful man in the community. Booker looks shocked and purports not to have ever heard of the fact that Bradley had a connection to Malcolm X.

Except that in the other interviews in the documentary, individuals repeatedly assert that everyone in the community knows about Bradley. They just choose to "leave it alone." However, instead of asking any follow up questions, the documentary moves on to other matters. It's incredible. They just let Booker off the hook as soon as they catch him on it.

Now normally there were a lot of police officers when Malcolm X spoke anywhere, but there were none on the day of the assassination. The lack of police presence was notable and the documentary has interviews with witnesses who confirm this. They also describe how lackadaisical the police were in their response afterward to the shooting.

What is glossed over is the fact that numerous FBI infiltrators were present in the Ballroom that day. One of them, John X. Ali, met with one of the shooters *the day before the shooting*. Another FBI man, Gene Roberts, was the man who got to the body of Malcolm X before anyone else and allegedly attempted CPR to revive him.[xxxviii] Meanwhile Betty Shabazz screamed and tried to get to her husband.

It is interesting that Roberts was the man who got Malcolm X first because it fits a pattern of other assassinations. Three years later, when Dr. Martin Luther King was murdered in Memphis, the first person to get to his body was an FBI informant named Marrell McCullough. McCullough later went on to work for the CIA.[xxxix] Then, in December 1969, when the Black Panther organized Fred Hampton was murdered by Chicago police, the man who drugged Hampton so he wouldn't wake up was the BPP treasurer and also, an FBI informant.[xl] When the assassinations take place, efforts are made to have the FBI asset confirm the deceased.

FINAL THOUGHTS

Malcolm X was killed at about 3 PM.

That night, the Audubon Ballroom was scheduled to host the George Washington Celebration.

Instead of canceling the event, the body was removed, the blood cleaned off the floor, and by 7 PM the party went on as scheduled. Four hours after he was killed, people were dancing literally on the spot he died. They danced in honor of George Washington.

Symbolism doesn't get any more obvious than that. Or, as Malcolm himself put it: "The job of the Negro civil rights leader is to make the Negro forget that the wolf and the fox both belong to the same family. Both are canines; and no matter which one of them the Negro places his trust in, he never ends up in the White House, but always the doghouse."[xli]

About a month before he was assassination, Malcolm met with the poet and activist Amir Baraka. In that meeting, Malcolm proposed that activists needed to concentrate on making "...politically viable a Black united front in the U.S." As Baraka points out: "This is the opposite of the religious sectarianism of the Nation of Islam. It is an admission that Islam is not the only road to revolutionary consciousness and that Muslims, Christians, Nationalists, and Socialists can be joined together as an antiimperialist force in the U.S.".[xlii]

Malcolm was opening up in that last year of his life, which terrified the reactionary elements in the U.S, government who arranged his assassination. Any documentary worth its salt has to take that as its starting point and move forward from there, because it is frankly obvious. It also becomes even more obvious when the greater context of the other assassinations, the movements, and the specific government operations for which voluminous documentary exists. The ultimate message of *Who Killed Malcolm X?* sacrifices clarity and context by treating the assassination like an ordinary murder, chasing individual suspects and missing the underlying political structures. Unfortunately, that means the six hours of this series wind up in failure, as for the most part it relies on the most unedifying aspects of the story.

But perhaps it's to be expected. It was always unlikely that Netflix was going to bankroll something that really rocks the boat. In fact, we know what happens to people who try. The filmmaker Louis Lomax, in 1968, who originally brought *The Hate that Hate Produced* to the attention of Mike Wallace in the Fifties, wanted to make a film about Malcolm X. A film in which the intelligence agencies, not the Nation of Islam, would be blamed for the murder. In other words, it was an attempt to make an *Executive Action*-style film, an extremely radical project.[xliii]

The film never got made. The brakes on Louis Lomax's car stopped functioning one day in July 1970. Lomax died in the resulting crash.[xliv] That too, alas, is familiar.

APPENDIX

THE PROPAGANDA DETECTION KIT
(26 PRINCIPLES FOR LIFE)

Go get the book PROPAGANDA by Jacques Ellul. Read it. You're gonna be able to use that for the rest of your life.

Read enough Marx to at least understand economic motives. That doesn't mean becoming a Marxist. That means that when Marx said we should pay attention to the economic motives that are behind the positions people take on issues, we should maybe pay attention to that. It's not deterministic; it's not that there are never exceptions. But generally speaking, as Whitey Herzog said, "If you take care of the percentages, the percentages will take care of you."

Remember that everyone has biases of one kind or another. That's not a slur, by the way. Having a bias just means you're human. Objectivity is neither possible nor desirable. I have biases. You do too. It's fine. You just have to know what they are.

Personal biases are less important, generally, than

151

functional biases. A functional bias, by my way of thinking, means that a person is representing more than just their personal opinion as a spokesperson. The Pope is going to say papal things, no matter who that pope happens to be. (Pope John Paul I tried to say different things and ended up dead 33 days later.) A guy representing Goldman Sachs is going to say stuff that doesn't hurt Goldman Sachs' bottom line. Institutional and corporate pressures are intense.

Knowing that, don't go overboard with it. Biases are influences but they don't overdetermine everything. Sometimes folks go off the reservation. Actually, evidence against interest is my favorite thing in the world. When someone says something that may damage their own social station by implication, there's a decent chance it is true. Robert MacNeil, the famous reporter who was part of the MacNeil-Lehrer Report for decades, risked some of his journalistic credibility when he pointed out that even the police ran onto the grassy knoll during the Kennedy assassination. (He was in Dealey Plaza when it happened.) "Why would they be fooled?" he said. That's a good observation, because it would be easier for him to play ball with the official story and he aired doubts anyway.

Values are completely screwed up in our society. On a scale of 0 to 100, the folks who do trash pickup are at 100 while any high school administrator is zero or less. Their monetary rewards do not match that importance.

And yet if you were introducing your new date to family or friends, would you be more comfortable introducing the principal or the sanitation engineer? Why? Because you're human.

Professional journalists and television shows will always paint people who research anything out of the ordinary as lunatics or idiots. This is in the aggregate - remember, there might be individuals who do not think this way; however, they are vastly outnumbered. More importantly, they are overpowered because everything in their profession is mitigating whatever values they are trying to maintain. One out of a thousand people will be able to resist this; most people just talk themselves into believing whatever the majority believes.

This one is a little weird. I've made this point before on radio interviews, and it still mostly works. You're going to notice that a lot of people who get interviewed on news programs went to what I call the three C's: Cornell, Columbia, and the University of Chicago. Part of it is that those are great schools, no doubt, but after a while you realize they always seem to be commenting on the same things and you know exactly what they're gonna say. You will start to pick up things like this if you start going down the researcher path in earnest.

As I discussed before, remember that the State isn't neutral. There is always a point of view that the State is trying to promulgate, which will be more or less successfully translated into the major media. Forget about democrat and republican, that's all shit. Remember the New York Times - "all the news that's fit to print." There are decisions made about which stories to hype and which to throw away. Invert the importance of those stories and you will be well on your way to finding out some truth.

This is an old Mae Brussell/John Judge trick: When something major happens - a terrorist attack, an assassination, a plane goes down with someone important on board - start that as day one and work through news stories backward. If the oil minister of Venezuela jumps off a hotel balcony, start going backward with news stories about the oil minister, about Venezuela, and start trying to see connections. Lay it out in front of yourself and you may find out some things.

Speaking of Mae Brussell, listen to as many of her shows as you can. My buddy Rob Falotico, RIP, created a website with tons of her content: worldwatchers.info. John Judge you can find videos of on the web. You can also find content at the Hidden History Center and Ratical.org.

The Washington Post is the CIA paper of record. That will explain a lot about what happens on its op-ed pages.

Remember that, in general, most politicians tend to

skew sociopathic. Every now and then there's a good one. You can tell those because they generally get murdered. (Although that isn't foolproof. Sometimes they end up as collateral damage to an operation. Allard Lowenstein took CIA money despite doing some good work on the RFK assassination, but that might have also gotten him killed, since he was shot by a guy who claimed the CIA had put a transmitter in his teeth. Seriously.) But guys like Walter Reuther, Congressman Leo Ryan, Paul Wellstone, those were good people. Reuther and Wellstone went down in planes. Ryan was shot to death during the Jonestown massacre.

Obviously, pay attention to small plane crashes. Go read *The Secret History of Airplane Sabotage* by Sherman Skolnick. Also check out the work of Rodney Stich.

Get politically active. You'll get your heart broken lots of times. Do it anyway. Cynicism is warranted and earned, but non-involvement also means ceding political decisions to the stupidest people in the country. Yes, I think voting is bullshit. I do it anyway. Putting less pressure on politicians doesn't help our cause.

I love universities. I love education. My pop is a retired professor and I grew up holding academia sacred. That having been said, the university has largely been ruined by the explosion of administrators. You'll find some good professors here and there, but the best thing about universities is the access to books. You don't need some guy to tell you what Rousseau said - he's available in the library. Read whatever you want, but I will suggest you read at least some of the authors that have proven to be valuable for thousands of years.

It's boring, but one thing to pay attention to is to read what powerful elites read. That means *Foreign Affairs* magazine. That also means *The Economist* and *The Financial Times*. You can sometimes learn what's coming next around the corner just by looking at those publications.

Don't get too excited about someone's YouTube video. A lot of crap gets posted there. Could be right, could be wrong, but you've got to verify it.

QAnon got started on message boards. The thing about message boards is you might find some interesting information, but you have to vet that information because 90% of everything is crap - as Gene Roddenberry observed. It's very easy to get caught up in something that lots of people are also getting excited about. Don't. Stay cool. Either something is true or it ain't. Making teams or getting into fights is a waste of time.

Researching this sort of thing is thankless. You might get the truth, but you also might get ostracized. Also, the truth sucks. It isn't good guys and bad guys, it's mostly bad guys with horrible motives who might occasionally find themselves as adversaries. I hate to be a downer, but it's how it is. On the other hand, what are you gonna do? Switch teams? Nah.

Don't get hung up on patriotism. As Paddy Chayefsky wrote in the famous speech delivered by Ned Beatty in *Network*, multinational corporations are the main players now.

Never trust anything said by rich guys favored by the media - i.e., Elon Musk, Bill Gates, etc. In any revolution those guys will be your enemies.

I don't put a lot of stock in Noam Chomsky, but he made a very good point when he said that democracies need propaganda a lot more than dictatorships. A dictator tells everybody what to do and they do it because or else. Democracies have to make things seem like they're on the up and up.

Hard binaries are a trap.

Almost nothing is simple. You'll know you're getting somewhere when everything feels like a mess and you're starting to think you'll never figure any of this out.

Read as much Robert Anton Williams as you can stand.

And good luck out there.

ABOUT THE AUTHOR

Joseph E. Green is the author of a zine series for Microcosm Publishing, including *What Happened to the Black Panthers?* and *An Intro to the Chappaquiddick Conspiracies*. He is the author of the books *Tinfoil Hat Not Included, Dissenting Views*, and *Dissenting Views II*. He is also the author of the plays *Clowntime is Over, The Vapours, The Dull are the Damned,* and *Einstein's Wrong About Everything*, as well as co-writing and co-producing a documentary, *King Kill 63*, featuring Oliver Stone, Dick Gregory, Richard Belzer, and Jesse Ventura, and served as the research consultant to Randy Benson's documentary film *The Searchers*.

joegreenjfk.com
saysomethingrealpress.org

[i] Rothschild, Mark. The Observer, "Why Twitter and Facebook are Powerless to Stop QAnon right now," 8/6/2020.

[ii] https://www.nationalreview.com/corner/the-breaking-of-stephen-colbert/, June 15, 2021.

[iii] *Betrayal: The Crisis in the Catholic Church*, 51.

[iv] Ibid, 131.

[v] Ibid, 176.

[vi] Koestler, Arthur, and J. R. Smythies, ed. *Beyond Reductionism: New Perspectives in the Life Sciences* (The Hutchinson Publishing Group: New York 1969), 310-311.

[vii] Postman, Neil, *Amusing Ourselves to Death* (Penguin Group: New York 1985), 36-37.

[viii] Turner, William, *Rearview Mirror* (Penmarin Books: Granite Bay, CA 2001). 6-7.

[ix] Rushkoff, Douglas, *Coercion* (Riverhead Books: New York, 1999), 67.

[x] Tuchman, Barbara, *The Guns of August*, 337.

[xi] Rampton, Shelton, & John Stauber, *Trust Us, We're Experts,* 41-45.

[xii] Ibid, 46-47.

[xiii] https://techcrunch.com/2019/08/28/youtube-to-reduce-conspiracy-theory-recommendations-in-the-uk/

[xiv] https://www.theguardian.com/commentisfree/2019/nov/11/democracy-defenders-economic-freedom-neoliberalism

[xv] Palast, Greg, *The Best Democracy Money Can Buy* (Penguin: New York 2003), 200.

[xvi] https://finance.yahoo.com/news/the-internet-is-at-a-real-crossroads-world-wide-web-foundation-ceo-160742193.html

[xvii] Staff and agencies in Geneva. "Fake Human Sacrifice Filmed at CERN, with Pranking Scientists Suspected." The Guardian (The Guardian), August 18, 2016. https://www.theguardian.com/science/2016/aug/18/fake--human--sacrifice--filmed--at--cern--with--pranking--scientists--suspected.

[xviii] Swanburg, W. A. *Citizen Hearst.* Scribner/Collier. New York, New York: 1961, p 528.

[xix] Varoufakis, Yanis, Joseph Halevi, and Nicholas Theocarakis. *Modern Political Economics: Making Sense of the Post-2008 World.* Routledge, 2012, p. 251.

ENDNOTES

[20] Gatto, John Taylor. "The Public School Nightmare." http://www.diablovalleyschool.org/nightmare.shtml.

[21] Saunders, Frances Stonor. "Modern Art Was CIA 'weapon.'" The Independent -- World (Independent), October 21, 1995. Accessed September 16, 2016. http://www.independent.co.uk/news/world/modern--art--was--cia--weapon--1578808.html.

[22] Parenti, Michael. *Dirty Truths* (City Lights Books: San Francisco, CA 1996).
[23] http://www.smh.com.au/articles/2002/04/24/1019441262517.html

[24] *Spooked*, 108
[25] https://consortiumnews.com/2014/10/16/kill-the-messenger-rare-truth-telling/

[26] DiEugenio, Jim, and Lisa Pease, ed. *The Assassinations* (Feral House: Los Angeles CA 2003), 404.

[27] Grant, Colin, "Negro With a Hat: The rise and fall of Marcus Garvey," *The Independent*, 10 February 2008. https://www.independent.co.uk/arts-entertainment/books/reviews/negro-with-a-hat-the-rise-and-fall-of-marcus-garvey-by-colin-grant-779373.html

[28] Powers, Richard, *The Life of J. Edgar Hoover: Secrecy and Power* (The Free Press: New York 1987), 50.

[29] Carson, Clayborne, *Malcolm X: The FBI File* (Carroll & Graf: New York 1991), 43.

[30] Evanzz, Karl, *The Judas Factor: The Plot to Kill Malcolm X* (Thunder's Mouth Press: New York), 73.

[31] Randeree, Bilal, "The Malcolm X Story Lives On," Alajazeera News, 28 April 2010. https://www.aljazeera.com/focus/2010/04/2010428135830700115.html

[32] Rafalko, Frank J., *MH/CHAOS: The CIA's Campaign Against the Radical New Left and the Black Panthers* (Naval Institute Press: Annapolis, MD 2011), 15.

[33] COINTELPRO documents link:

https://www.freedomarchives.org/Documents/Finder/Black%20Liberation%20Disk/Black%20Power!/SugahData/Government/COINTELPRO.S.pdf

[xxxiv] Evanzz, 172.

[xxxv] Evanzz, 175.

[xxxvi] DiEugenio and Pease, 396.

[xxxvii] Marable, Manning, *Malcolm X: A Life of Reinvention* (Viking: New York 2011), 475.

[xxxviii] Marable, 439.

[xxxix] DiEugenio, Jim, "The 13th Juror," (review).
https://kennedysandking.com/martin-luther-king-reviews/the-13th-juror

[xl] Green, Joseph E. "The Open Assassination of Fred Hampton,"
https://ratical.org/ratville/JFK/FredHampton.html

[xli] X, Malcolm, *The End of White World Supremacy* (Arcade Publishing: New York 2011), 137.

[xlii] Baraka, Amir, "Malcolm as Ideology," *Malcolm X in Our Own Image* (St. Martin's Press: New York 1992), 29.

[xliii] Canby, Vincent, "Two Studios Plan Malcolm X Films: James Baldwin and Louis Lomax writing scripts," *The New York Times*, 8 March 1968.

[xliv] Evanzz, 319.

www.ingramcontent.com/pod-product-compliance
Lightning Source LLC
Chambersburg PA
CBHW060015050426
42448CB00012B/2756